Siân Davies is a barrister at 39 Essex Chambers with experience across the range of legal issues encountered by adult social services (including mental capacity), children's services and housing departments, and is particularly experienced at dealing with cases involving immigration, asylum and EU law and the impact of such status upon access to services. She provides advice, representation and training to individuals, local authorities and health bodies and is a part time Judge of the First tier Tribunal (Mental Health).

A Practical Guide to the Availability of Local Authority Support for People from Abroad

A Practical Guide to the Availability of Local Authority Support for People from Abroad

Siân Davies
Barrister, Gray's Inn
MA (Oxon) LLM

Law Brief Publishing

Published 2022 by Law Brief Publishing, an imprint of Law Brief Publishing Ltd
30 The Parks
Minehead
Somerset
TA24 8BT

www.lawbriefpublishing.com

Paperback: 978-1-914608-24-7

For all my wonderful family, and
particularly Andy, Hayley and Isabella –
thank you for your love and support

PREFACE

Lord Hoffmann observed, in the case of *Westminster CC v NASS* [2002] UKHL 38, that, "*there was a time when the welfare state did not look at your passport or ask why you were here … As immigration became a political issue, this changed*" [19-20].

The legal landscape in relation to immigration has become deeply political, and a consequence of that has been increased regulation regarding the ability of those from abroad to access state support, whether in the form of central or local government provision.

Such change continues to take place: there have been key legislative changes in 2002, 2014, 2016 and 2020 (the latter to reflect the UK's departure from the European Union). More legislative change is underway, in the form of the Nationality and Borders Bill which has received Royal Assent on 28 April 2022.

Many important parts of the welfare state are therefore subject to immigration related qualifying or disqualifying criteria. The affected provisions include the benefits administered by central government and some (but not all) of the social welfare schemes which are the responsibility of local government.

The result is that those seeking support from a local authority, and those responsible for administering the provision of local authority services such as housing, social care, emergency relief, public health and assistance to children, are increasingly required to understand not just the statutory schemes under which such assistance is granted or denied, but also the immigration landscape which forms the backdrop to those schemes.

The purpose of this book is to seek to identify the key areas where local government support and immigration status collide, and to assist those seeking and administering support to navigate those areas.

The law stated in this book is believed to be correct as of 29th April 2022.

Siân Davies
May 2022

CONTENTS

CHAPTER ONE

WHAT DOES 'NO RECOURSE TO PUBLIC FUNDS' (NRPF) MEAN?

1.1 NRPF has become a generic description for what is in reality a relatively diverse group of immigration statuses.

1.2 It derives from the provisions of the Immigration Rules, which at para.6, define "public funds". Those which fall within the ambit of English local government administration are in bold (emphasis added):

(a) **housing under Part VI or VII of the Housing Act 1996** and under Part II of the Housing Act 1985, Part I or II of the Housing (Scotland) Act 1987, Part II of the Housing (Northern Ireland) Order 1981 or Part II of the Housing (Northern Ireland) Order 1988; and

(b) attendance allowance, severe disablement allowance, carer's allowance and disability living allowance under Part III of the Social Security Contribution and Benefits Act 1992; income support, council tax benefit and housing benefit under Part VII of that Act; a social fund payment under Part VIII of that Act; child benefit under Part IX of that Act; income based jobseeker's allowance under the Jobseekers Act 1995, income related allowance under Part 1 of the Welfare Reform Act 2007 (employment and support allowance) state pension credit under the State Pension Credit Act 2002; or child tax credit and working tax credit under Part 1 of the Tax Credits Act 2002; and

(c) attendance allowance, severe disablement allowance, carer's allowance and disability living allowance under Part III of the Social Security Contribution and Benefits (Northern Ireland) Act

2.13 EEA nationals, and their family members, who:

1. have acquired limited leave to enter and remain in the UK (also known as pre-settled status) by virtue of Appendix EU of the Immigration Rules ("the EU Settlement Scheme"); or

2. were frontier working in the UK prior to 31 December 2020

will continue to be treated as NSTIC in line with their pre-Brexit status, and therefore Reg.6 of the Eligibility Regulations applies in such cases.

2.14 Whether an EEA national (or family member) has exercised a right to reside in the UK or rights to be treated as a frontier worker will depend on their circumstances at that particular time. For example, whether the EEA national is, for the purposes of the Immigration (European Economic Area) Regulations 2016 ('the EEA Regulations') (as preserved by the savings provisions) a jobseeker, a worker, a self-employed person and so on.

Settled and pre-settled status of EEA nationals

2.15 Applications to the EUSS scheme are decided by reference to Appendix EU to the Immigration Rules.

2.16 Broadly speaking, an EEA national who was in the UK at 11pm on 31 December 2020 and who had, or qualified for, a permanent right of residence under the Immigration (European Economic Area) Regulations 2016, would be granted settled status. That would be a person who was able to evidence having exercised a right – for example as a worker, self-employed person, or family member of a "qualified person" for five years. The EEA qualified person was under no obligation to obtain a residence permit, and even if a residence permit had been obtained, it has been held to be evidence of a right to reside as a matter of EU law, rather than the source of lawful presence under EU law (in contrast to a visa, for example): see *Dias v Secretary of State* [2009] EWCA Civ 807. So for many EEA nationals applying under the EUSS scheme,

CHAPTER ONE

WHAT DOES 'NO RECOURSE TO PUBLIC FUNDS' (NRPF) MEAN?

1.1 NRPF has become a generic description for what is in reality a relatively diverse group of immigration statuses.

1.2 It derives from the provisions of the Immigration Rules, which at para.6, define "public funds". Those which fall within the ambit of English local government administration are in bold (emphasis added):

(a) **housing under Part VI or VII of the Housing Act 1996** and under Part II of the Housing Act 1985, Part I or II of the Housing (Scotland) Act 1987, Part II of the Housing (Northern Ireland) Order 1981 or Part II of the Housing (Northern Ireland) Order 1988; and

(b) attendance allowance, severe disablement allowance, carer's allowance and disability living allowance under Part III of the Social Security Contribution and Benefits Act 1992; income support, council tax benefit and housing benefit under Part VII of that Act; a social fund payment under Part VIII of that Act; child benefit under Part IX of that Act; income based jobseeker's allowance under the Jobseekers Act 1995, income related allowance under Part 1 of the Welfare Reform Act 2007 (employment and support allowance) state pension credit under the State Pension Credit Act 2002; or child tax credit and working tax credit under Part 1 of the Tax Credits Act 2002; and

(c) attendance allowance, severe disablement allowance, carer's allowance and disability living allowance under Part III of the Social Security Contribution and Benefits (Northern Ireland) Act

1992; income support, council tax benefit and, housing benefit under Part VII of that Act; a social fund payment under Part VIII of that Act; child benefit under Part IX of that Act; income based jobseeker's allowance under the Jobseekers (Northern Ireland) Order 1995 or income related allowance under Part 1 of the Welfare Reform Act (Northern Ireland) 2007; and

(d) Universal Credit under Part 1 of the Welfare Reform Act 2012 or Personal Independence Payment under Part 4 of that Act; and

(e) Universal Credit, Personal Independence Payment or any domestic rate relief under the Welfare Reform (Northern Ireland) Order 2015; and

(f) **a council tax reduction under a council tax reduction scheme made under section 13A of the Local Government Finance Act 1992** in relation to England or Wales or a council tax reduction pursuant to the Council Tax Reduction (Scotland) Regulations 2012 or the Council Tax Reduction (State Pension Credit) (Scotland) Regulations 2012; and

(g) a payment made from a welfare fund under the Welfare Funds (Scotland) Act 2015; and

(h) a discretionary support payment made in accordance with any regulations made under article 135 of the Welfare Reform (Northern Ireland) Order 2015; and

(i) **a discretionary payment made by a local authority under section 1 of the Localism Act 2011.**

[**emphasis added to identify those forms of support administered by an English local authority**]

1.3 It can be seen that the majority of the welfare provisions defined as public funds are those administered by central government.

1.4 It is also notable that key local authority welfare provisions are *not* within the definition of public funds – support under the Children Act 1989, Care Act 2014 and after-care under the Mental Health Act 1983, for example. Some of those schemes contain their own immigration related eligibility criteria. However, they are not "public funds" as defined and the mere fact that an applicant is subject to a NRPF condition on their leave to enter or remain does not exclude them from such forms of support.

Who has "NRPF"?

1.5 The umbrella term NRPF is capable of including those who have been granted leave to enter or leave to remain, where the grant is subject to a condition of NRPF. That applicant is *lawfully present* in the UK, but the condition precludes access to the specified forms of support.

1.6 An unlawfully present person (someone who has overstayed a visa, for example, or a failed asylum seeker who has exhausted all appeal rights) might also be described as having NRPF. An EEA national who does not have settled or pre-settled status or leave to remain would also be unlawfully present and unable to qualify for the specified forms of welfare assistance, therefore NRPF. That is because such qualification is in all cases dependent on lawful presence in the UK (among other conditions).

1.7 An asylum seeker is a person who is subject to immigration control and therefore requires, but (pending a positive decision on the asylum claim and consequential grant of leave to remain) does not have, leave to remain. Asylum seekers' needs are addressed by the Immigration and Asylum Act 1999 s.95, which permits the Secretary of State to provide accommodation and support for destitute asylum seekers. An asylum seeker therefore has NRPF by reference to mainstream welfare support, but may be able to access public funds in the form of asylum support.

Key points

- NRPF is an umbrella term which covers those who, either because their presence is unlawful, or because it is lawful but subject to conditions, may not have access to public funds

- An asylum seeker is excluded from access to public funds but, if destitute, may qualify for support from the Home Office under s.95 Immigration and Asylum Act 1999

- Local authority support provisions which include the Care Act 2014, Children Act 1989 and Mental Health Act 1983 are outside the definition of "public funds" (but may have their own statutory immigration restrictions)

CHAPTER TWO

ELIGIBILITY UNDER THE HOUSING ACT 1996 (HA 1996)

2.1 A key issue in relation to local authority support for persons from abroad is access to accommodation/housing. The main legislative scheme dealing with local authority accommodation is the Housing Act 1996. As will be seen, it contains provisions which limit access to housing via the allocations route as well as entitlement to support as a homeless person by reference to a person's immigration status.

Key legislative provisions

2.2 For the purposes of Part 6 HA 1996, the key provision is s.160ZA "*Allocation only to eligible and qualifying persons*". This provision states, materially, that:

> (1) A local housing authority in England shall not allocate housing accommodation—
>
> (a) to a person from abroad who is ineligible for an allocation of housing accommodation by virtue of subsection (2) or (4), or
>
> (b) to two or more persons jointly if any of them is a person mentioned in paragraph (a).
>
> (2) A person subject to immigration control within the meaning of the Asylum and Immigration Act 1996 is ineligible for an allocation of housing accommodation by a local housing authority in England unless he is of a class prescribed by regulations made by the Secretary of State.
>
> (3) No person who is excluded from entitlement to universal credit or housing benefit by section 115 of the Immigration

and Asylum Act 1999 (exclusion from benefits) shall be included in any class prescribed under subsection (2).

(4) The Secretary of State may by regulations prescribe other classes of persons from abroad who are ineligible to be allocated housing accommodation by local housing authorities in England.

...

The section operates by drawing a division between those who are "subject to immigration control" ("STIC") and those who are "not subject to immigration control" ("NSTIC"). Those who are STIC are ineligible for an allocation of housing accommodation from a local housing authority unless they are of a prescribed class and thereby "*re-qualify*": s.160ZA (2). A person who is NSTIC is eligible, unless removed from eligibility by Regulations, as permitted by s.160ZA (4).

It is necessary also to consider, by reference to s.160ZA (4), the Allocation of Housing and Homelessness (Eligibility) (England) Regulations (SI 1296/2004) ("the Eligibility Regulations").

2.3 Regulation 3 of the Eligibility Regulations allows specified classes of person STIC to re-qualify as eligible. Those classes are:

(a) Class A — a person who is recorded by the Secretary of State as a refugee within the definition in Article 1 of the Refugee Convention and who has leave to enter or remain in the United Kingdom;

(b) Class B — a person—

(i) who has exceptional leave to enter or remain in the United Kingdom granted outside the provisions of the Immigration Rules; and

(ii) who is not subject to a condition requiring him to maintain and accommodate himself, and any person who is dependent on him, without recourse to public funds;

(c) Class C — a person who is habitually resident in the United Kingdom, the Channel Islands, the Isle of Man or the Republic of Ireland and whose leave to enter or remain in the United Kingdom is not subject to any limitation or condition, other than a person—

(i) who has been given leave to enter or remain in the United Kingdom upon an undertaking given by his sponsor;

(ii) who has been resident in the United Kingdom, the Channel Islands, the Isle of Man or the Republic of Ireland for less than five years beginning on the date of entry or the date on which his sponsor gave the undertaking in respect of him, whichever date is the later; and

(iii) whose sponsor or, where there is more than one sponsor, at least one of whose sponsors, is still alive; [...]

(d) Class D— a person who has humanitarian protection granted under the Immigration Rules

(f) Class F – a person—

(i) who has limited leave to enter or remain in the United Kingdom on family or private life grounds under Article 8 of the Human Rights Convention that is granted under paragraph 276BE(1), paragraph 276DG or Appendix FM of the Immigration Rules; and

(ii) who is not subject to a condition requiring the person to maintain and accommodate himself, and any person dependent upon him, without recourse to public funds;

(g) Class G – a person who is habitually resident in the United Kingdom, the Channel Islands, the Isle of Man or the Republic of Ireland and who has been transferred to the

United Kingdom under section 67 of the Immigration Act 2016 and has limited leave to remain under paragraph 352ZH of the Immigration Rules

(h) Class H – a person who is habitually resident in the United Kingdom, the Channel Islands, the Isle of Man or the Republic of Ireland and has Calais leave to remain under paragraph 352J of the Immigration Rules

(i) Class I – a person (P) who has limited leave to enter or remain in the United Kingdom by virtue of Appendix EU of the Immigration Rules in circumstances where—

(i) P is a family member of a relevant person of Northern Ireland ("RP") in accordance with those rules; and

(ii) P would have been considered eligible under regulation 4(2)(d) if RP were a person specified in regulation 4(2)(a) to (c) ;

(j) Class J – a person who is habitually resident in the United Kingdom, the Channel Islands, the Isle of Man or the Republic of Ireland and who has limited leave to remain in the United Kingdom as a stateless person under paragraph 405 of the Immigration Rules

(k) Class K – a person (P)—

(i) who has limited leave to enter or remain in the United Kingdom by virtue of Appendix Hong Kong British National (Overseas) of the Immigration Rules;

(ii) whose leave to enter or remain is not subject to a condition requiring P to maintain and accommodate P, and any person dependent upon P, without recourse to public funds; and

(iii) who is habitually resident in the United Kingdom, the Channel Islands, the Isle of Man or the Republic of Ireland

(l) Class L – a person—

(i) who is granted leave to enter or remain in the United Kingdom in accordance with the Immigration Rules, where such leave is granted by virtue of—

(aa) the Afghan Relocations and Assistance Policy; or

(bb) the previous scheme for locally-employed staff in Afghanistan (sometimes referred to as the ex-gratia scheme); or

(ii) with leave to enter or remain in the United Kingdom not coming within sub-paragraph (i), who left Afghanistan in connection with the collapse of the Afghan government that took place on 15th August 2021, but excluding a person (P)—

(aa) who is subject to a condition requiring P to maintain and accommodate themself, and any person who is dependent on P, without recourse to public funds; or

(bb) who has been given leave to enter or remain in the United Kingdom upon an undertaking given by P's sponsor and has been resident in the United Kingdom, the Channel Islands, the Isle of Man or the Republic of Ireland for less than five years beginning on the date of entry or the date on which P's sponsor gave the undertaking in respect of P, whichever date is the later, and whose sponsor or, where there is more than one sponsor, at least one of whose sponsors, is still alive.

2.4 New regulations (in force on 22 March 2022) address the eligibility for housing and homelessness assistance of people who have left Ukraine as a result of the Russian invasion. The relevant statutory Instrument affecting this change is the Allocation of Housing and Homelessness (Eligibility) (England) and Persons subject to Immigration Control (Housing Authority Accommodation and Homelessness) (Amendment) Regulations 2022 (SI.No.339/2022), the effect of which is to amend the Allocation of Housing and Homelessness (Eligibility) (England) Regulations 2006 (SI.No.1294/2006) so that local authorities in England can treat as eligible for housing and homelessness assistance people who -

- left Ukraine as a result of the Russian invasion on 24 February 2022 and had resided in Ukraine immediately before 1 January 2022; and
- have been granted leave in accordance with the Immigration Rules made under section 3(2) of the Immigration Act 1971 (the explanatory memorandum to the regulations advises that the Home Office will amend their Immigration Rules to reflect the 36-month limited leave to remain that is available under the Ukraine Family Scheme and the Homes for Ukraine scheme).

In relation to those who meet the residence and immigration conditions outlined above, the regulations recognise that British citizens who resided in Ukraine may have been forced to leave because of the circumstances of the invasion, and so such persons (who are NSTIC) are exempt from the habitual residence test.

2.5 Those who are NSTIC are eligible unless removed from eligibility by Reg.4 of the Eligibility Regulations. The main qualification to the eligibility of a NSTIC person is whether he is "habitually resident" in the UK, Channel Islands, Isle of Man or Republic of Ireland[1]. However, the habitual residence test does not apply to a person who is a worker, self-employed person, or "qualified person" for the purposes of the Immigration (European Economic Area) Regulations 2006.

2.6 A habitually resident person whose only right to reside is as a jobseeker, family member of a jobseeker or is an EEA initial right to reside is nonetheless not eligible.

---

[1] Known as the "Common Travel Area"

2.7 A person who is not habitually resident is also eligible if they fall within the classes specified in Reg.3(2). Such persons include a person granted a right to reside under Appendix EU of the Immigration Rules (these are the post-Bexit Immigration Rules which deal with applications for leave to remain under the EU Settled Status Scheme ("EUSS").

Part 7 Housing Act 1996 – homelessness assistance

2.8 The key statutory provision is s.185 HA 1996 "*persons from abroad not eligible for housing assistance*" which states that:

> (1) A person is not eligible for assistance under this Part if he is a person from abroad who is ineligible for housing assistance.
>
> (2) A person who is subject to immigration control within the meaning of the Asylum and Immigration Act 1996 is not eligible for housing assistance unless he is of a class prescribed by regulations made by the Secretary of State.
>
> (2A) No person who is excluded from entitlement to universal credit or housing benefit by section 115 of the Immigration and Asylum Act 1999 (exclusion from benefits) shall be included in any class prescribed under subsection (2).
>
> (3) The Secretary of State may make provision by regulations as to other descriptions of persons who are to be treated for the purposes of this Part as persons from abroad who are ineligible for housing assistance.
>
> (4) A person from abroad who is not eligible for housing assistance shall be disregarded in determining for the purposes of this Part whether a person falling within subsection (5)—
>
> (a) is homeless or threatened with homelessness, or
>
> (b) has a priority need for accommodation.

(5) A person falls within this subsection if the person—

(a) falls within a class prescribed by regulations made under subsection (2); but

(b) is not a person who, immediately before IP completion day, was—

(i) a national of an EEA State or Switzerland, and

(ii) within a class prescribed by regulations made under subsection (2) which had effect at that time.

2.9 As with s.160ZA, there are two categories of applicant. Those who are STIC are ineligible unless able to re-qualify by Regulations, see s.185(2). Those who are NSTIC are eligible unless disqualified by regulations. The relevant Regulations are the Eligibility Regulations at Reg. 5 (those STIC who are able to re-qualify) and 6 (disqualifying certain categories of those NSTIC). These replicate the categories discussed above in relation to allocations (Regs 3 and 4): see 2.3 and 2.4 above.

2.10 Chapter 7 of the Homelessness Code of Guidance addresses eligibility.

Who is subject to immigration control?

2.11 The Court of Appeal considered this in *LB Barnet v Ismail and others* [2006] EWCA Civ 383. It held at para.4 that "subject to immigration control":

> ...is, for the purposes of section 185(2) of the Housing Act, to be interpreted according to section 13(2) of the Asylum and Immigration Act 1996: a person is so subject to immigration control if he is "a person who under [the Immigration Act 1971] **requires leave to enter or remain in the United Kingdom (whether or not such leave has been given)**". The terms of section 13(2) of the 1996 Act can only be understood in the context of the Immigration Act 1971,

> which underpins them and, as we have seen, is specifically referred to in the 1996 Act. The scheme of the 1971 Act was, put shortly, that **only persons having the right of abode in the United Kingdom are free to live in and come and go to and from this country. By section 1(2) of the Act, other persons may only live in the United Kingdom with permission and subject to such regulation as the Act provides.** The advent of the European Union required special arrangements to be made for nationals of member states of the Union, such as are the present respondents; but those arrangements are still within the framework of and subject to the assumptions of the 1971 Act. Those special arrangements are to be found in section 7 of the Immigration Act 1988. That provides that a person does not require leave under the 1971 Act to enter or remain in the United Kingdom if he is entitled to enter or remain in the United Kingdom "by virtue of an enforceable Community right or of any provision made under section 2(2) of the European Communities Act 1972." The respondents do not assert (or in the unusual structure of this case it might be more accurate to say, do not admit to) any enforceable Community right, but reference must be made to the relevant provision made under section 2(2), the Immigration (European Economic Area) Regulations 2000. [Emphasis added]

2.12 Post-Brexit, certain categories of EEA national continue to be NSTIC. The provisions of section 7(1) of the Immigration Act 1988 and the Asylum and Immigration Act 1996 have been saved for the purpose of housing legislation to protect the rights of EEA nationals, and their family members, who have citizens' rights pursuant to the Withdrawal Agreement[2].

---

[2] Agreement on the Withdrawal of the United Kingdom of Great Britain and Northern Ireland from the European Union and the European Atomic Energy Community [TS No.3/2020]

2.13 EEA nationals, and their family members, who:

1. have acquired limited leave to enter and remain in the UK (also known as pre-settled status) by virtue of Appendix EU of the Immigration Rules ("the EU Settlement Scheme"); or

2. were frontier working in the UK prior to 31 December 2020

will continue to be treated as NSTIC in line with their pre-Brexit status, and therefore Reg.6 of the Eligibility Regulations applies in such cases.

2.14 Whether an EEA national (or family member) has exercised a right to reside in the UK or rights to be treated as a frontier worker will depend on their circumstances at that particular time. For example, whether the EEA national is, for the purposes of the Immigration (European Economic Area) Regulations 2016 ('the EEA Regulations') (as preserved by the savings provisions) a jobseeker, a worker, a self-employed person and so on.

Settled and pre-settled status of EEA nationals

2.15 Applications to the EUSS scheme are decided by reference to Appendix EU to the Immigration Rules.

2.16 Broadly speaking, an EEA national who was in the UK at 11pm on 31 December 2020 and who had, or qualified for, a permanent right of residence under the Immigration (European Economic Area) Regulations 2016, would be granted settled status. That would be a person who was able to evidence having exercised a right – for example as a worker, self-employed person, or family member of a "qualified person" for five years. The EEA qualified person was under no obligation to obtain a residence permit, and even if a residence permit had been obtained, it has been held to be evidence of a right to reside as a matter of EU law, rather than the source of lawful presence under EU law (in contrast to a visa, for example): see *Dias v Secretary of State* [2009] EWCA Civ 807. So for many EEA nationals applying under the EUSS scheme, it was necessary to produce documentary evidence establishing that the right to reside had been exercised for the required period.

2.17 An EEA national who was exercising an EEA free movement right but did not qualify for (or could not evidence) the five years of status would qualify for pre-settled status, which is capable of being converted to settled status at the five year mark, subject to confirmation that the free movement rights have continued to be exercised.

2.18 As a matter of EU law, certain third country (i.e. non-EEA) nationals are able to establish EEA rights of residence, usually because of a relationship, such as primary carer or spouse, to an EEA national. These third country rights continue into the EUSS scheme and include:

- a third country relative who used to have an EU, EEA or Swiss family member living in the UK but this relationship is no longer subsisting, for example due to separation or death

- a third country relative of a British citizen, if they lived outside the UK in an EEA country together

- a third country relative of a British citizen who also has EU, EEA or Swiss citizenship and who lived in the UK as an EU, EEA or Swiss citizen before getting British citizenship

- a third country primary carer of a British, EU, EEA or Swiss citizen

- a third country relative who is the child of an EU, EEA or Swiss citizen who used to live and work in the UK, or who is the child's primary carer

2.19. A '*Zambrano* carer' is a non-EEA national parent or carer (so a third country national) of a dependent British citizen child, where the British citizen would be unable to reside in the UK if the carer had to leave. Following the European Court of Justice's decision in *Ruiz Zambrano v Office National de l'Emploi* (C-34/09) [2012] QB 265, *Zambrano* carers have been recognised to have a right to reside under EU law. This recognition was reflected in amendments to the Immigration (European Economic Area) Regulations 2016.

2.20 The EUSS scheme excluded anyone who already had leave to remain on another basis (for example on private and family life grounds under Article 8 ECHR). This exclusion was applicable to a *Zambrano* carer, and likely to have wider application to persons with this category of residence right, for the practical reason that leave to remain on article 8 grounds is capable of being granted *with recourse to public funds*, whereas "mere" *Zambrano* status does not carry entitlement to most forms of welfare assistance, or to homelessness assistance under the Housing Act 1996.

It is therefore a viable practical option for a person who qualified for *Zambrano* carer status to apply for leave to remain on article 8 ECHR grounds (there being overlap between the Zambrano requirements i.e. primary carer of a citizen child) and establishing private and family life in the UK. If article 8 ECHR leave to remain was granted initially subject to a NRPF condition, it was possible to apply for this condition to be removed if there was evidence of actual or imminent destitution: see chapter 6 in relation to such applications.

A grant of settled status is not subject to a NRPF condition, and there is no cost for renewal of settled status (in contrast to leave to remain).

2.21 In *Akinsanya v Secretary of State for the Home Department* [2022] EWCA Civ 37 the Court of Appeal held that the exclusion of a *Zambrano* carer from the EUSS scheme if the carer had leave to remain was unlawful by reference to Reg.16 of the Immigration (European Economic Area) Regulations 2016, which implemented the *Zambrano* right to reside in domestic legislation. So, while the SoS was found correctly to have interpreted the scope of the *Zambrano* right under EU law (i.e. as being limited to the situation where the carer has no domestic or other EU right of residence), the EUSS scheme required to be redrafted.

Late Applications to the EUSS scheme

2.22 Certain applicants can continue to apply to the scheme (in addition to the discretion to accept late applications) for example a person whose visa expired after 30 June 2021[3].

What is "habitual residence"?

2.23 Annex 1 of the Homelessness Code of Guidance[4] addresses the habitual residence test ("HRT"). It states that there is no definition of habitual residence and that all circumstances are to be taken into account. The guidance advises that:

(a) the test focuses on the fact and nature of residence;

(b) a person who is not resident somewhere cannot be habitually resident there. Residence is a more settled state than mere physical presence in a country. To be resident a person must be seen to be making a home. It need not be the only home or a permanent home but it must be a genuine home for the time being. For example, a short stay visitor or a person receiving short term medical treatment is not resident;

(c) the most important factors for habitual residence are the length, continuity and general nature of actual residence rather than intention;

(d) the practicality of a person's arrangements for residence is a necessary part of determining whether it can be described as settled and habitual;

(e) established habitual residents who have periods of temporary or occasional absence of long or short

---

3 https://www.gov.uk/settled-status-eu-citizens-families/eligibility

4 https://www.gov.uk/guidance/homelessness-code-of-guidance-for-local-authorities/annex-1-the-habitual-residence-test

duration may still be habitually resident during such absences.

Both intentions and actions are to be investigated, and it is suggested that such inquiries are appropriate if the applicant has been in the UK for less than 2 years. A person who leaves another country does not become habitually resident immediately on arrival, even if s/he came here voluntarily with the intention to settle. The applicant must be resident in fact for an appropriate period of time which demonstrates that residence has become, and is likely to remain, habitual in nature (see: *Nessa v Chief Adjudication Officer* [1999] UKHL 41). However, the situation is different if a person is returning to the UK having previously resided in the UK and now seeking to re-establish residence.

2.24 There are two main requirements to establish habitual residence:

- residence must be for an 'appreciable period of time'
- there must be an intention to settle in the UK.

The statutory guidance requires consideration of where the applicant's "centre of interest" lies [Annex 1, para.19]. This concept is said to include:

(a) home;

(b) family ties;

(c) club memberships;

(d) finance accounts.

2.25 The concepts of normal, ordinary and habitual residence feature in a number of statutory schemes and have therefore been the subject of considerable judicial consideration.

R v London Borough of Barnet Ex parte Shah [1983] 2AC 309, is a case addressing ordinary residence. Lord Scarman said at 343 G-H:

> Unless, therefore, it can be shown that the statutory framework or the legal context in which the words are used requires a different meaning, I unhesitatingly subscribe to the view that ordinarily resident refers to a man's abode in a particular place or country which he has adopted voluntarily and for settled purposes as part of the regular order of his life for the time being, whether of short or of long duration.

The legal landscape on the issue of habitual residence is summarised in the judgment of Charles J. in R(Greenwich) v SoS Health[5]. The following points were taken from an extensive overview of the legal authorities:

(a) the words used, **whether the word before residence is ordinary, normal or habitual**, are ordinary English words and the decision maker can determine by applying their ordinary meaning to the facts of a given case what the answer is

(b) as recorded in paragraph 18 of the judgment in *Mohamed v London Borough of Hammersmith and Fulham* [2002] 1AC 1487, the ordinary English words and their application may take meaning from their context.

(c) ordinary residence connotes residence in a place with some degree of continuity and apart from accidental or temporary absences.

(d) Enforced presence may be so overwhelming a factor as to negative the will to be where one is. Examples include kidnap or imprisonment.

(e) There need not be an intention to stay indefinitely. The settled purpose may be for a limited period. All that is necessary is that the purpose of living where one does has a

[5] https://www.bailii.org/ew/cases/EWHC/Admin/2006/2576.html

sufficient degree of continuity to be properly described as settled.

Mohamed v Hammersmith London Borough Council [2002] 1 AC 547 concerned whether accommodation provided as temporary accommodation by a housing authority was capable of giving rise to normal residence.

Paragraph 18 of the speech of Lord Slynn sets out the clear position that a temporary placement is capable of giving rise to ordinary or normal residence:

> It is clear that words like 'ordinary residence' and 'normal residence' may take their precise meaning from the context of the legislation in which they appear but it seems to me that the prima facie meaning of normal residence is a place where at the relevant time the person in fact resides. That therefore is the question to be asked and it is not appropriate to consider whether in a general or abstract sense such a place would be considered an ordinary or normal residence. **So long as that place where he eats and sleeps is voluntarily accepted by him, the reason why he is there rather than somewhere else does not prevent that place from being his normal residence. He may not like it, he may prefer some other place, but that place is for the relevant time the place where he normally resides. If a person, having no other accommodation, takes his few belongings and moves to a barn for a period to work on a farm that is where during that period he is normally resident, however much he might prefer some more permanent or better accommodation. In a sense it is 'shelter' but it is also where he resides. Where he is given interim accommodation by a local housing authority even more clearly is that the place where for the time being he is normally resident.** The fact that it is provided subject to statutory duty does not, contrary to the appellant's authority's argument, prevent it from being such."

In *Al-Ameri v RB Kensington and Chelsea* [2004] UKHL 4 the applicants were former asylum seekers who had been provided with accommodation in Glasgow by the Home Office's National Asylum Support Service under the Immigration and Asylum Act 1999. They were then granted leave to remain, and were required to leave the NASS accommodation, but by virtue of having leave to remain were eligible for assistance under Part 7 Housing Act 1996, and made an application to RB Kensington and Chelsea as homeless persons. The decision on that application was that while the authority was satisfied as to homelessness, eligibility for assistance, and priority need, and was not satsideied that there was intentional homelessness, it was determined that the conditions for referral to Glasgow City Council under s198(1) of the 1996 Act were met.

Section 198(2) Housing Act 1996 allows an authority to refer an applicant to another authority where three conditions are met: (a) neither the applicant nor any person who might reasonably be expected to reside with him has a local connection with the authority's district; (b) the applicant or a person who might reasonably be expected to reside with him has a local connection with the district of the other authority; and, (c) neither the applicant nor any person who might reasonably be expected to reside with him will run the risk of domestic violence in that other district. Local connection is defined in s199(1).

By s199(1)(a), 'a person has a local connection with a district if he is, or in the past was, normally resident there, and that residence is or was of his own choice'.

The issue before the Court was to whether asylum seekers dispersed under the NASS scheme had choice as to where they resided. It was held that they had no choice, as the place in which they were accommodated was at the Secretary of State's direction. The asylum-seeker's only choice was between going where he was directed by the NASS scheme and homelessness, which was held not to amount to a choice for the purposes of s199(1)(a).

The House of Lords' decision was subsequently reversed by amendment to s.199 Housing Act 1996 which now provides that:

> (6) A person has a local connection with the district of a local housing authority if he was (at any time) provided with accommodation in that district under section 95 of the Immigration and Asylum Act 1999 (support for asylum seekers).
>
> (7) But subsection (6) does not apply—
>
> (a) to the provision of accommodation for a person in a district of a local housing authority if he was subsequently provided with accommodation in the district of another local housing authority under section 95 of that Act, or
>
> (b) to the provision of accommodation in an accommodation centre by virtue of section 22 of the Nationality, Immigration and Asylum Act 2002 (c. 41) (use of accommodation centres for section 95 support).

The case is nonetheless instructive in terms of consideration of whether and when accommodation will be regarded as not being voluntarily adopted.

Housing Eligibility and EEA nationals

EEA citizens who resided in the UK before 31 December 2020

2.26 The Withdrawal Agreement protects the rights of EEA citizens and their family members who were lawfully residing, or frontier working, in the UK before 11pm on 31 December 2020, including access to social housing and homelessness assistance.

2.27 An application was required to be made to the EU Settlement Scheme ("EUSS") before the deadline of 30 June 2021[6].

---

[6] Late applications to the scheme are permitted in limited circumstances see https://www.gov.uk/settled-status-eu-citizens-families/eligibility

Late applications are also potentially valid if there are reasonable grounds for the application being late - see https://assets.publishing.service.gov.uk/government/uploads/system/uploads/attachme

2.28 An applicant who is granted *settled status* under the EUSS has the same access to social housing and homelessness assistance as a comparable British citizen. They should be eligible provided they can demonstrate habitual residence in the Common Travel Area, under provisions in Regulation 3(c) and Regulation 5(1)(c) of the Eligibility Regulations i.e STIC, but with unlimited and unconditional leave to remain.

2.29 An applicant granted *pre-settled status* is or frontier working in the UK will be subject to the eligibility criteria under Regulations 4 (for allocations) and 6 (for homelessness assistance) of the Eligibility Regulations. Whether the pre-settled applicant is eligible or not will depend on what he is doing, in terms of exercising what were formerly EEA Treaty rights, in the UK. So, for example, the pre-settled worker will be eligible for assistance (Reg.4(2) and 6(2)) whereas the pre-settled jobseeker will be ineligible (Reg.4(1) and 6(1)).

EEA citizens moving to the UK from 1 January 2021

2.30 Those EEA citizens who enter the UK after 1 January 2021 are treated in the same way as non-EEA persons from abroad, i.e. under the Immigration Rules, and require leave to enter or leave to remain. Such leave will generally be granted on the condition of no recourse to public funds, which will therefore preclude access to social housing and homelessness assistance.

2.31 The exceptions to that position are:

(a) the family member who is joining an EEA citizen who was residing in the UK before 31 December 2020.

(b) Irish nationals, who are treated in the same way as a British citizen.

---

nt_data/file/1041794/EU_Settlement_Scheme_EU_other_EEA_Swiss_citizens_and_family_members.pdf

(c) A person whose status enables them, although STIC, to re-qualify as eligible for assistance, for example because they have been granted refugee status, or indefinite leave to remain.

What inquiry is required into a person's immigration status when an application is made for housing assistance?

2.32 One of the core difficulties in relation to identifying the powers and duties available to a local authority in relation to a person from abroad lies in the complexity of the immigration system, the multiple types of status a person might be granted (some of which carry a NRPF condition) and the levels of review and appeal an applicant might encounter on their journey through the immigration system. For housing officers, and social workers concerned with the needs of adults and children, and for applicants themselves, identifying immigration status for the purposes of working out consequential entitlement to local authority support is far from straightforward.

2.33 The duty to make inquiries under the Housing Act 1996 Part 7 is addressed in s.184 (1) which states that:

> (1) If the local housing authority have reason to believe that an applicant may be homeless or threatened with homelessness, **they shall make such inquiries as are necessary to satisfy themselves—**
>
> (a) **whether he is eligible for assistance**, and
>
> (b) if so, whether any duty, and if so what duty, is owed to him under the following provisions of this Part.
>
> (2) They may also make inquiries whether he has a local connection with the district of another local housing authority in England, Wales or Scotland.
>
> (3) On completing their inquiries the authority shall notify the applicant of their decision and, so far as any issue is decided against his interests, inform him of the reasons for their decision.

2.34 The level of inquiry is identified as that which is necessary for the local authority to be satisfied as to the applicant's eligibility. The extent of the duty to make inquiries is a matter for the local housing authority, and it has been held that the Court should not intervene unless satisfied that *no reasonable housing authority could have been satisfied on the basis of the inquiries made*; see R v Royal Borough of Kensington and Chelsea, ex p Bayani (1990) 22 H.L.R. 406 and R(on the application of Khatun) v Newham London BC (Office of Fair Trading, interested party) [2004] EWCA Civ 55.

2.35 In *R(Burns) v LB Southwark* [2004] EWHC 1901 (Admin) the applicant was a third country national who relied upon her status as the spouse of an EEA worker to establish her NSTIC status (and therefore eligibility under Part 7). Her argument was that in exercising its discretion to accommodate her pending review under section 188(3), the local authority was required to inquire into her status in the UK and assess for itself what status she was entitled to on the basis of the evidence before it, and that the issue of her eligibility under Part 7 could not lawfully be determined without doing so. The counter argument was that the local authority was entitled to rely on a decision of the Secretary of State for the Home Department refusing the applicant an EEA residence permit under the Immigration (European Economic Area) Regulations 2000.

It was held, in relation to the relative expertise of housing officers and the Home Office, that the "Home Office European Union unit which will have more experience on such matters" [41] and on the core issue of whether it was unreasonable for the local authority to rely upon the Secretary of State's decision:

In my judgment, it cannot be unreasonable for the defendant in such a case, and in particular in this case, to have relied on the evidence of the Secretary of State's refusal [42].

2.36 Note that the Code of Guidance at 7.33 advises contacting the Home Office if there is uncertainty about the immigration status of any household member of a Part 7 applicant. While that is the obvious starting point in relation to any uncertainty as to the status of an applicant or household member, the responsiveness of the Home Office to such queries is not necessarily consistent with the timescales required for consideration of a homelessness application, particularly where there is an urgent need for housing.

Restricted cases under Part 7

2.37 A restricted case is a case where the housing authority would not be satisfied that the applicant had a "priority need" for accommodation (defined by s.189) without having regard to a 'restricted person' within the household. So, priority need is capable of being conferred if there is a dependent child in the household, but if the applicant is NSTIC, does not have priority need in his own right, but the dependent child relied upon for priority need is ineligible, e..g. because he needs but does not have leave to ender or remain in the UK, or has leave to enter subject to a NRPF condition, the dpendent child is a "restricted person".

2.48 In a restricted case, the housing authority must, so far as reasonably practical, bring the section 193(2) duty to an end by arranging for an offer of an assured shorthold tenancy to be made to the applicant by a private landlord (a private rented sector offer of at least 12 months in length).

The Homelessness Code of Guidance at 7.33 advises that:

> Where a housing authority considers a household member of an applicant may be a restricted person who does not have leave to enter or remain in the UK, or if there is uncertainty about the immigration status of any household member, it is recommended that the authority contact the Home Office.

Obtaining information about an applicant's status

A local authority can subscribe to *NRPF connect*[7], which is a secure online database holding information about the immigration status of an applicant for support. The systems enable a local authority user to identify whether applications are pending (and ought therefore to be prioritised by the Home Office if local authority support is being

[7] https://www.nrpfnetwork.org.uk/nrpf-connect

provided, per para.85 of *Clue v Birmingham CC*), and whether there have been, or are currently, presentations to other local authority areas seeking support.

Key points

- **A person who is STIC is ineligible, unless able to "re-qualify" under the Eligibility Regulations**

- **A person who is NSTIC is eligible, unless disqualified by the Eligibility Regulations**

- **EEA nationals who were in the UK before 31 December 2020 were (and in certain situations are) able to apply to the EUSS scheme for settled or pre-settled status, which operates as a grant of leave to remain**

- **EEA nationals entering the UK after 31 December 2020 are treated in the same way as those from non-EEA countries (unless joining an EEA family member)**

- **Third country (non-EEA) nationals who had an EU right of residence can apply to the EUSS scheme**

- **An "ineligible person" as defined by Schedule 3 NIAA 2002 may not be provided with (discretionary) accommodation pending statutory review or statutory appeal, unless (and to the extent that) such accommodation is necessary to prevent a breach of a person's human rights, because of the prohibition in para.1(1)(j) of Schedule 3.**

- **The duty to make inquiries into an applicant's eligibility is to make those inquiries necessary to satisfy the local authority, which is capable of being challenged if the inquiry made (or not made) was irrational. Statutory guidance is that in a case of uncertainty as to status, the Home Office should be contacted.**

CHAPTER THREE

THE CARE ACT 2014

3.1 Where a person is assessed as having eligible needs, either for care and support themselves or as a carer, where certain conditions are met, a duty arises upon the local authority to meet those needs (s.18 in relation to the service user, and s.20 in relation to the carer).

3.2 By section 21, there is an exception in the case of a person subject to immigration control. This states that:

> (1) A local authority may not meet the needs for care and support of an adult to whom section 115 of the Immigration and Asylum Act 1999 ("the 1999 Act") (exclusion from benefits) applies and whose needs for care and support have arisen solely—
>
> (a) because the adult is destitute, or
>
> (b) because of the physical effects, or anticipated physical effects, of being destitute.
>
> (2) For the purposes of subsection (1), section 95(2) to (7) of the 1999 Act applies but with the references in section 95(4) and (5) to the Secretary of State being read as references to the local authority in question.
>
> (3) But, until the commencement of section 44(6) of the Nationality, Immigration and Asylum Act 2002, subsection (2) is to have effect as if it read as follows—
>
> "(2) For the purposes of subsection (1), section 95(3) and (5) to (8) of, and paragraph 2 of Schedule 8 to, the 1999 Act apply but with references in section 95(5) and (7) and that paragraph to the Secretary of State being read as references to the local authority in question."

> (4) The reference in subsection (1) to meeting an adult's needs for care and support includes a reference to providing care and support to the adult in order to meet a carer's needs for support.

3.3 This prohibition extends to the prevention duty (s.2 Care Act 2014) by virtue of s.21(5) which amends s.2 in the case of a person excluded from benefits on immigration grounds by re-drafting s.2(1) to state that:

> (1) A local authority may not perform the duty under section 2(1) in relation to an adult to whom section 115 of the Immigration and Asylum Act 1999 ("the 1999 Act") (exclusion from benefits) applies and whose needs for care and support have arisen, or for whom such needs may in the future arise, solely—
>
> (a) because the adult is destitute, or
>
> (b) because of the physical effects, or anticipated physical effects, of being destitute.", and
>
> (b) subsection (4) were omitted.

Who is STIC for the purposes of s.21?

3.4 This is discussed elsewhere, and is in fact a wider class of person than those to whom s.115 of the Immigration and Asylum Act 1999 applies. The prohibition on providing care and support, carer support or services to prevent care and support needs arising is limited to those to whom s.115 applies. Section 115 defines a person STIC as:

> (9) *"A person subject to immigration control"* means a person who—
>
> (a) **requires leave to enter or remain in the United Kingdom but does not have it;**
>
> (b) has leave to enter or remain in the United Kingdom which is **subject to a condition that he does not have recourse to public funds;**

(c) has leave to enter or remain in the United Kingdom given as a result of a **maintenance undertaking**; …

A maintenance undertaking is defined at s.115(10) as "…a written undertaking given by another person in pursuance of the immigration rules to be responsible for that person's maintenance and accommodation".

"Destitute plus"

3.5 The prohibition on providing Care Act 2014 support to those STIC (as defined) is limited to those whose actual or anticipated need is solely because of destitution or its actual or anticipated physical effects. The same condition applied to the predecessor legislation to the Care Act 2014, in the form of s.21(1A) of the National Assistance Act 1948. Under the NAA 1948 it was held that the need for care and attention (the criteria for s.21(1)(a) NAA support) must to a material extent be made more acute by age, illness, disability or any other circumstances (those being the applicable reasons as to why care and attention must be required for s.21(1)(a) NAA purposes): see *R(O) v LB Wandsworth*.

Does the need arise solely from destitution?

3.6 This question would arise only once it was established that there was a need (for care and support, under the Care Act 2014)

3.7 According to the House of Lords in *M v Slough BC* [2008] UKHL 52, the first question is whether there is a need which *goes beyond the need for shelter and subsistence*. If so:

If… that state of need has been accelerated by some pre-existing disability or infirmity – not of itself sufficient to give rise to a need for care and attention but such as to cause a faster deterioration to that state and perhaps to make the need once it arises that much more acute – then, for my part… I would not regard such a person as excluded [40(ii)]

3.8 It has been held that mental illness is capable of being a physical effect of destitution. In *R(PB) v LB Haringey* [2006] EWHC 2255 (Admin) at [49] it was held that the local authority had failed to consider in its assessment whether the depression from which the applicant was acknowledged to be suffering arose *solely from destitution*, or whether there was another cause of the mental illness in addition to her destitution. A depressive illness arising solely from destitution would preclude the availability of support, whereas a depressive illness attributable to some other cause would not preclude local authority support.

3.9 It should be recalled that the destition is defined by s.95 of the Immigration and Asylum Act 1999, as meaning that a person does not have adequate accommodation or any means of obtaining it (whether or not other essential living needs are being met); or if he or she does have adequate accommodation or has the means of obtaining it, but cannot meet other essential living needs.

Interplay with Schedule 3 NIAA 2002

3.10 The section 21 Care Act 2014 prohibition is in addition to the prohibition on the provision of support under Part 1 of the Care Act to an "ineligible person" per para.1 (1) (n) of Schedule 3 NIAA 2002. Even if the s.21 prohibition does not apply (e.g. because the need is not solely attributable to destitution), the service user may be ineligible for care and support because of the application of Schedule 3.

3.11 There are therefore in effect two immigration related hurdles that a person STIC has to overcome in relation to the Care Act 2014 in order to be provided with support, (in addition to the criteria for support which apply irrespective of immigration status, such as there being assessed eligible needs, and ordinary residence or no settled residence).

Key points

- **A person to whom a care and support duty, duty to a carer, or prevention duty is owed, may be ineligible to receive such support if they are unlawfully in the UK (or have an immigration condition that excludes access to public funds) AND the need has arisen solely because of destitution or its actual or anticipated physical effects;**

- The prohibition on meeting needs includes providing support to the adult (service user) in order to meet needs of a carer (e.g. for respite);
- The s.21 prohibition is in addition to Schedule 3 NIAA 2002. In the case of a person STIC with care and support needs, it would need to be established that neither the s.21 prohibition of Schedule 3 ineligibility applies.

CHAPTER FOUR

ELIGIBILITY UNDER THE NATIONALITY IMMIGRATION AND ASYLUM ACT 2002 (NIAA)

The statutory scheme

4.1 Section 54 of the NIAA gives effect to Schedule 3.

4.2 Paragraph 1 of Schedule 3 sets out the prohibited forms of support. It provides that a person to whom para.1 applies shall not be eligible for support and assistance under the specified statutory provisions. By para.1(2), the specified powers and duties "may not be exercised or performed in respect of a person to whom this paragraph applies (whether or not the person has previously been in receipt of support or assistance under the provision)". The specified provisions are:

> (c) section 12 or 13A of the Social Work (Scotland) Act 1968 (c. 49) (social welfare services),
>
> (d) Article 7 or 15 of the Health and Personal Social Services (Northern Ireland) Order 1972 (S.I. 1972/1265 (N.I. 14)) (prevention of illness, social welfare, &c.),
>
> [...]
>
> (f) section 29(1)(b) of the Housing (Scotland) Act 1987 (c. 26) (interim duty to accommodate in case of apparent priority need where review of a local authority decision has been requested),
>
> (g) [section 17, 23C, 23CZB, 23CA, 24A or 24B of the Children Act 1989 (c. 41)]3 (welfare and other powers which can be exercised in relation to adults),

(h) Article 18, 35 or 36 of the Children (Northern Ireland) Order 1995 (S.I. 1995/755 (N.I. 2)) (welfare and other powers which can be exercised in relation to adults),

(i) sections 22, 29 and 30 of the Children (Scotland) Act 1995 (c. 36) (provisions analogous to those mentioned in paragraph (g)),

(j) section 188(3) or 204(4) of the Housing Act 1996 (c. 52) (accommodation pending review or appeal),

(k) section 2 of the Local Government Act 2000 (c. 22) (promotion of well-being),

(ka) section 1 of the Localism Act 2011 (local authority's general power of competence),

(l) a provision of the Immigration and Asylum Act 1999 (c. 33) ,

(m) a provision of this Act

(n) Part 1 of the Care Act 2014 (care and support provided by local authority)

(o) Part 4 (duty of local authority to meet needs) or sections 105 to 116 (leaving care, accommodation and fostering) of the Social Services and Well-being (Wales) Act 2014.

4.3 So far as England is concerned, the prohibited forms of support are:

- section 17 Children Act 1989 (but only insofar as an adult is concerned) as this provision permits the provision of support to a child in need and to his family, see s.17(3) "Any service provided by an authority in the exercise of functions conferred on them by this section may be provided for the family of a particular child in need or for any member of his family, if it is provided with a view to safeguarding or promoting the child's welfare"

- section 23C, 23CZB, 23CA, 24A or 24B of the Children Act 1989. These provisions relate to support for care leavers, i.e. those over 18 who were looked after children and qualify for leaving care support

- section 188(3) Housing Act 1996 which permits (but does not require) a local housing authority to accommodate an applicant for homelessness assistance pending a statutory review of a decision as to what, if any, duty is owed under Part 7 of that Act

- section 204 (4) Housing Act 1996 which permits (but does not require) a local housing authority to accommodate an applicant for homelessness assistance pending a statutory appeal under s.204 against a s.202 review decision

- section 2 of the Local Government Act 2000 which grants a power to a local authority to do anything likely to promote economic, social or environmental well-being of their area

- Section 1 of the Localism Act 2011, which is the general power of competence to a local authority (discussed further in chapter 9 in relation to its application to persons from abroad)

- The Immigration and Asylum Act 1999

- The NIAA 2002

- Part 1 of the Care Act 2014, which includes the assessment provisions for both service user and carer, and the powers and duties to meet assessed eligible needs.

4.4 While the prohibited forms of support are wide-ranging and include housing assistance (to the extent that it is not already subject to the eligibility provisions of the Housing Act 1996), care and support and support for adults and support under the Children Act 1989, as well as the more general discretionary powers, it is important to note that *not every form of statutory support which is capable of including accommodation is prohibited.*

4.5 Examples of accommodation powers and duties which are *not* within the prohibited forms of support are:

(a) Section 117 Mental Health Act 1983: After-care under s.117 of the Mental Health Act 1983 is capable of including the provision of accommodation, and is not subject to any immigration related restriction. However, it is clear from case law that the circumstances in which ordinary accommodation can be provided by way of after-care, irrespective of any immigration related consideration, are limited.

In *R (Mwanza) v LB of Greenwich* [2010] EWHC 1462 (Admin) the claimant was an illegal overstayer (therefore unlawfully present, and not an asylum seeker) who relied upon a detention under s.3 of the Mental health Act 1983 some eight years earlier as a basis for seeking accommodation from the local authority. It was held that (1) An after-care service under s117 must be a service that is necessary to meet a need arising from a person's mental disorder. It does not cover any and all services simply because those services do or may prevent deterioration of relapse of a mental condition. There was a distinction between those needs common to all which do not arise from mental disorder, although mental disorder may give rise to a need for assistance in meeting them. As a matter of law, ordinary accommodation could fall within s117, although it was held to be difficult readily to envisage any practical examples, and s.21 National Assistance Act 1948 (the predecessor to the Care Act 2014) was a "far more appropriate vehicle for requiring authorities to provide mere housing, than the provisions relating to mental health" [78]. Section 21 was, by the provisions of Schedule 3 then in force, one of the prohibited forms of support for the purposes of Schedule 3, and it was held that the Schedule prohibited the provision of accommodation under s.21 to the claimant because of his status as an ineligible person and the availability of a relocation abroad as a means of avoiding a breach of human rights.

The circumstances in which after-care is capable of including accommodation are limited, and the scope for accommodation under this provision is further discussed in *R(Afework) v LB*

Camden [2013] EWHC 1637 (Admin). Mostyn J. held at [19] that:

...as a matter of law s117(2) is only engaged vis-à-vis accommodation if:

(i) The need for accommodation is a direct result of the reason that the ex-patient was detained in the first place ("the original condition");

(ii) The requirement is for enhanced specialised accommodation to meet needs directly arising from the original condition; and

(iii) The ex-patient is being placed in the accommodation on an involuntary (in the sense of being incapacitated) basis arising as a result of the original condition.

(b) Local Government Act 1972 s.138 powers in relation to disaster and emergency

As discussed below, in *R(Ncube) v Brighton and Hove CC* it was held that emergency powers under s.138 of the Local Government Act 1972 in relation to disasters and emergencies, are capable of giving rise to a power to accommodate those without lawful immigration status.

(c) Section 2B of the National Health Service Act 2006

This is a target duty (and so does not give rise to an individual enforceable right) but is capable of permitting the provision of accommodation, for example in a rehabilitation facility, or in a night shelter under a severe weather protocol, without reference to immigration status, on public health grounds (see *Ncube*).

The Care Act 2014

4.6 Schedule 3 para.1(n) specifies the whole of Part 1 of the Care Act 2014 as a prohibited form of support. Part 1 includes the assessment provisions in relation to an adult "Where it appears to a local authority that an adult may have needs for care and support". Under s.10 of the 2014 Act there is a duty to assess the needs of a carer "Where it appears to a local authority that a carer may have needs for support (whether currently or in the future)...".

4.7 Those assessment provisions (as well as the service provisions in the event that eligible needs are identified) are on the face of it prohibited by para.1(1) (n) of Schedule 3. There are two possible approaches to this. The first is that an assessment is not "support or assistance" but is a precursor to the provision of such support or assistance. The second is that, in any case where a local authority is prohibited from providing support, the prohibition is disapplied if, and to the extent that, the support or assistance is necessary to prevent a breach of a person's human rights (para.3). If the extent of a person's care and support needs (or needs as a carer) are not known because there has not been an assessment, it is difficult to see how there could be a lawful determination as to what, if any, support or assistance is required to prevent a breach of human rights. The care and support needs assessment may be a necessary procedural step in the course of a human rights assessment.

Exceptions to the prohibition

4.8 By paragraph 2 of Schedule 3, the prohibition does not apply to a British Citizen or to a child.

4.9 By paragraph 3 of Schedule 3, there is an exception to the prohibition on human rights grounds. This states that:

Paragraph 1 does not prevent the exercise of a power or the performance of a duty if, and to the extent that, its exercise or performance is necessary for the purpose of avoiding a breach of— (a) a person's Convention rights.

4.10 It is paragraph 3 which gives rise to the need for a human rights assessment in a case where a person is ineligible to be provided with support. While the Schedule itself contains no requirement for such an assessment, it is the mechanism by which a local authority is able to satisfy itself as to whether it is necessary (and the extent to which it is necessary) to exercise a prohibited power or duty to prevent a breach of human rights.

The classes of ineligible person

Refugee Status Abroad

4.11 By para.4 of Schedule 3:

> (1) Paragraph 1 applies to a person if he—
>
> (a) has refugee status abroad, or
>
> (b) is the dependant of a person who is in the United Kingdom and who has refugee status abroad.
>
> (2) For the purposes of this paragraph a person has refugee status abroad if—
>
> (a) he does not have the nationality of an EEA State [and is not a British citizen], and
>
> (b) the government of an EEA State has determined that he is entitled to protection as a refugee under the Refugee Convention.

This provision appears to be aimed at ensuring that those with refugee status granted by an EEA State (and their dependents) seek support and assistance from the State which has granted them such status, rather than from the UK.

The second class of ineligible person was (pre-Brexit) a citizen of an EEA State other than the UK. Such persons now fall to have their eligibility determined by reference to the remaining classes of ineligible person.

Failed asylum seeker

By para.6 of Schedule 3

> (1) Paragraph 1 applies to a person if—
>
> (a) he was (but is no longer) an asylum-seeker, and
>
> (b) he fails to cooperate with removal directions issued in respect of him.
>
> (2) Paragraph 1 also applies to a dependant of a person to whom that paragraph applies by virtue of sub-paragraph (1).

4.12 In *R(AW) v LB Croydon* [2005] EWHC 2950 (Admin) Lloyd-Jones J. considered whether failed asylum seekers were exclusively provided for at para. 6 of Schedule 3, or whether a failed asylum seeker who had not failed to co-operate with removal directions could nonetheless be ineligible under some other provision of the Schedule. It was concluded that para.6 had not been intended to make exclusive provision for failed asylum seekers, and that such a person might therefore not be ineligible under para.6 but nonetheless be ineligible under another class:

> 19. To my mind, there is nothing in the scheme or language of Schedule 3 to support the view that paragraph 6 was intended to make exclusive provision for failed asylum seekers to the exclusion of other categories of ineligibility. On the contrary, there appears to be no good reason why a failed asylum seeker who is not ineligible by virtue of paragraph 6 may not be ineligible on another ground. Thus, for example, a failed asylum seeker may not be ineligible within paragraph 6 because he has not failed to cooperate with removal directions, but may nevertheless be ineligible within paragraph 4 because he has refugee status abroad.

4.13 Person unlawfully in the UK who is not an asylum seeker

Para.7 of the Schedule states that:

Paragraph 1 applies to a person if—

(a) he is in the United Kingdom in breach of the immigration laws within the meaning of [section 50A of the British Nationality Act 1981, and

(b) he is not an asylum-seeker.

"in the United Kingdom in breach of the immigration laws"

This aspect of ineligibility is by reference to s.50A of the British Nationality Act 1981 which in turn provides at 50A (4) that:

(4) A person is in the United Kingdom in breach of the immigration laws if (and only if) the person—

(a) is in the United Kingdom;

(b) does not have the right of abode in the United Kingdom within the meaning of section 2 of the Immigration Act 1971;

(ba) is not an Irish citizen who does not require leave to enter or remain in the United Kingdom (see section 3ZA of the Immigration Act 1971);

(c) does not have leave to enter or remain in the United Kingdom (whether or not the person previously had leave);

...

(f) is not entitled to enter and remain in the United Kingdom by virtue of section 8(1) of the Immigration Act 1971 (crew) (whether or not the person was previously entitled); and

(g) does not have the benefit of an exemption under section 8(2) to (4) of that Act (diplomats, soldiers and other special cases) (whether or not the person previously had the benefit of an exemption).

4.15 A British or Irish citizen, or a person with a right of abode[8], does not require leave to enter or leave to remain in the UK. Other categories of person, unless exempt or crew, require such leave, and if they do not have it, will be in breach of the immigration laws as defined.

4.16 Prior to 15 January 2018[9], an asylum seeker could be granted "temporary admission". This was not a form of leave to enter of remain, merely an alternative to immigration detention. Nonetheless, if granted at port of entry, it could prevent the asylum seeker from being regarded as "*in* the UK" for the purposes of para.7 of Schedule 3. The status of "temporary admission" no longer exists and immigration bail is routinely granted to asylum seekers, albeit that this is not the same as the immigration bail which is capable of being granted to a person released from immigration detention.

4.17 "Not an asylum seeker"

The definition of an asylum seeker is contained in s.94 of the Immigration and Asylum Act 1999. An "asylum seeker" must be:

- Over 18
- Have made a claim for asylum which has been recorded by the Secretary of State but which has not been determined;
- A "claim for asylum" means a claim that it would be contrary to the United Kingdom's obligations under the Refugee Convention, or under Article 3 of the Human Rights Convention, for the claimant to be removed from, or required to leave, the United Kingdom

[8] All British and some Commonwealth citizens have a right of abode

[9] Immigration Act 2016, section 61

- A claim for asylum is determined either when the applicant is notified by the Secretary of State of a decision on the claim for asylum, or, if applicant has appealed against the Secretary of State's decision, on the day on which the appeal is disposed of i.e. there is no further appeal pending, or no further in-time right of appeal.

4.18 As noted in *R(AW) v LB Croydon*, a person may *have been* an asylum seeker but nonetheless qualify as ineligible under para.7 if there is no longer an extant claim for asylum. In *R(Mustafa) v Kent CC* [2018] EWHC 2025 (Admin) it was held that a person who has made further submissions to the Home Office in the hope that these will be accepted as a valid fresh claim for asylum by reference to para.353 of the Immigration Rules[10] is not an asylum seeker while a decision is awaited from the Home Office as to whether the further submissions meet the test so as to be treated as a valid fresh claim.

The Schedule 3 scheme: an overview

4.19 The starting point is to consider whether the statutory support the applicant is seeking is a form of support prohibited by para. 1 of Schedule 3. If it is not, further consideration is not required.

---

[10] Para.353 states that "When a human rights or protection claim has been refused or withdrawn or treated as withdrawn under paragraph 333C of these Rules and any appeal relating to that claim is no longer pending, the decision maker will consider any further submissions and, if rejected, will then determine whether they amount to a fresh claim. The submissions will amount to a fresh claim if they are significantly different from the material that has previously been considered. The submissions will only be significantly different if the content:

1. (i) had not already been considered; and
2. (ii) taken together with the previously considered material, created a realistic prospect of success, notwithstanding its rejection. This paragraph does not apply to claims made overseas".

4.20 The second relevant consideration is whether the applicant falls within the para.2 exceptions: are they a child or a British Citizen? If so, further consideration is not required.

4.21 The third consideration is whether the applicant falls within a class of ineligible person, by virtue of refugee status of an EEA state, being a failed asylum seeker who has failed to comply with removal directions, or being unlawfully in the UK (and not an asylum seeker). If the applicant is seeking a form of prohibited support, and is ineligible, the prohibition will apply unless (and to the extent that) support is necessary to avoid a breach of a person's human rights (para.3).

4.22 Para.7A contains a further class of ineligible person - a failed asylum seeker with a dependent child to whom the Secretary of State has issued a certificate confirming that the applicant has failed without reasonable excuse to leave the UK. That provision was part of a pilot scheme by which failed asylum seekers were issued with such certificates as a means of attempting to promote voluntary returns. The scheme is no longer in operation.

The future: additional classes of ineligible person

4.23 Para.7B (not yet in force[11]) provides for a sixth class of ineligible person who requires leave to enter or remain under the Immigration Act 1971 but does not have it, and who is not an asylum seeker, or the dependent of such a person.

4.24 Para.7C (also not in force) sets out a further class of ineligible person:

> (1) Paragraph 1 applies to a person in England ("P") if—
>
> (a) P is the primary carer of a British citizen ("the relevant British citizen"),

[11] Added by Immigration Act 2016

(b) the relevant British citizen is residing in the United Kingdom,

(c) the relevant British citizen would be unable to reside in the United Kingdom or in another EEA State if P were required to leave the United Kingdom,

(d) if circumstances were not as mentioned in paragraphs (a) to (c), under the Immigration Act 1971 P would require leave to enter or remain in the United Kingdom but would not have such leave, and

(e) P is not an asylum-seeker.

(2) Paragraph 1 also applies to the dependant of a person to whom that paragraph applies by virtue of sub-paragraph (1).

(3) In making for the purposes of this Schedule or regulations made under it a determination as to whether sub-paragraph (1)(c) applies in relation to P, a person may rely on—

(a) a document of a kind specified in regulations made by the Secretary of State, or

(b) information or guidance provided by the Secretary of State for the purposes of such a determination.

4.25 The description of this class of ineligible person closely matches the criteria for a person to qualify as a *Zambrano*[12] carer under EU law.

---

12 A 'Zambrano carer' is a non-EEA national parent or carer of a dependent British citizen child, where the British citizen would be unable to reside in the UK if the carer had to leave: *Ruiz Zambrano v Office National de l'Emploi* (C-34/09) [2012] QB 265. The Zambrano judgment was given effect in UK law by way of amendment to the Immigration (European Economic Area) Regulations 2016. The ability of Zambrano carers to apply for leave to remain under the EUSS scheme was considered by the Court of Appeal in *Akinsanya v SSHD* [2022] EWCA Civ 37

Asylum seeker with dependent child

4.26 Section 94 of the Immigration and Asylum Act 1999 defines an asylum seeker as including an asylum seeker whose household includes a child who is under 18 and a dependant of the asylum seeker. The asylum seeker is to be treated (for the purposes of this Part VI of the 1999 Act) as continuing to be an asylum-seeker while the child is under 18; and he and the child remain in the United Kingdom.

4.27 This is important in relation to the division of responsibility as between central and local government because central government is responsible for meeting the accommodation and subsistence needs of asylum seekers (as defined by s.94) under s.95 of that Act, and by s.122 (5) of the 1999 Act, a local authority is **prohibited** from providing support under the child welfare provisions of the Children Act 1989 in circumstances where the SoS is complying with s.95, or where there are reasonable grounds for believing that the applicant is a person for whom support may be provided under section 95 and the Secretary of State would be required to comply with s.95 if that person had made an application for section 95 support. If there are reasonable grounds for believing that the s.95 criteria are met, i.e. the applicant appears to be destitute[13], the prohibition on support under the Children Act 1989 to the family would apply.

4.28 The prohibited support (in England) is limited to s.17 of the Children Act 1989 (local authority support for children and their families). There is no prohibition on other forms of support under the CA 1989.

[13] S.95 (3) defines that as

(a)he does not have adequate accommodation or any means of obtaining it (whether or not his other essential living needs are met); or

(b)he has adequate accommodation or the means of obtaining it, but cannot meet his other essential living needs.

Key Points

- Schedule 3 NIAA 2002 para.1 sets out prohibited forms of support and assistance: a local authority may not provide these to an ineligible person

- The classes of ineligible person include a person with refugee status abroad, a failed asylum seeker who has failed to comply with removal directions, and a person who is unlawfully in the UK and who is not an asylum seeker

- EEA nationals are no longer a separate class of ineligible person, but potentially fall within other classes

- An ineligible person's exclusion from support is subject to the exceptions at paragraphs 2 and 3 of Schedule 3

- Paragraph 3 requires assessment of whether and to what extent support is necessary to prevent a breach of a person's human rights

- There is no prohibition on the provision of support to a child or a British Citizen

CHAPTER FIVE

AGE ASSESSMENT AND DUTIES TO CHILDREN UNDER THE CHILDREN ACT 1989

5.1 A destitute adult asylum seeker will (absent care and support needs, discussed further below) generally be supported by central government while a claim for asylum is being considered. A child arriving in the UK as an asylum seeker will meet the criteria for the provision of local authority support under s.20 of the Children Act 1989 and for the duration of that support will be a "looked after child" ("LAC").

The Children Act 1989

5.2 An Age Assessment is carried out by a local authority when seeking to determine whether to provide services to individuals under the Children Act 1989 ("CA 1989").

5.3 Section 17(1) of the CA 1989 provides:

> It shall be a general duty of every Local Authority,
>
> a) To safeguard and promote the welfare of children within their area who are in need;
>
> b) So far as is consistent with that duty, to promote the upbringing of such children by their families,
>
> by providing a range and level of services appropriate to those children's needs.

5.4 Section 20 of the CA 1989, entitled "*Provision of accommodation for children: general*", provides that:

> (1) Every local authority shall provide accommodation for any child in need within their area who appears to

them to require accommodation as a result of –

a) there being no person who has parental responsibility for him;

b) his being lost or having been abandoned (…).

5.5 An unaccompanied asylum seeking or refugee child without anyone having parental responsibility for them will invariably be regarded as a "*child in need*". There follows a duty upon the local authority, pursuant to sections 17 and 20 of the Children Act 1989 to provide accommodation and support to such a child.

5.6 Child is defined at s.105 of the Children Act 1989 as a person under the age of eighteen. Section 105(1) of the Children Act 1989 defines "child" as meaning a person under the age of eighteen.

Statutory Guidance

5.7 Care of Unaccompanied Migrant Children and Child Victims of Modern Slavery (November 2017)[14] is statutory guidance (see para.6) which is issued pursuant to section 7 of the Local Authority Social Services Act 1970. That brings into play the obligation upon a local authority to "act under" the guidance which has been held to require that it be complied with, unless there are cogent reasons for departure.

5.8 Paragraph 1 of the Statutory Guidance states that:

> "*Unaccompanied migrant children and child victims of modern slavery, including trafficking, can be some of the most vulnerable children in the country. Unaccompanied children are alone, in an unfamiliar country and may be surrounded by people unable to speak their first language. Modern slavery includes human trafficking, slavery, servitude and forced or compulsory labour. Exploitation takes a number of forms, including sexual exploitation, forced labour, forced criminality, begging, organ*

[14]https://assets.publishing.service.gov.uk/government/uploads/system/uploads/attachment_data/file/656429/UASC_Statutory_Guidance_2017.pdf

> *harvesting and domestic servitude and victims may come from all walks of life."*

5.9 Paragraph 35 of the Statutory Guidance is headed "*Age determination*" and states as follows:

> "*Many unaccompanied and trafficked children arrive in the UK without documentation or with forged or counterfeit documents. Where the age of a person is uncertain and there are reasons to believe they are a child, that person is presumed to be a child in order to receive immediate access to assistance, support and protection in accordance with section 51 of the Modern Slavery Act 2015. Where an age assessment is required, local authorities must adhere to standards established within case law. Age assessments should only be carried out where there is reason to doubt that the individual is the age they claim. Age assessments should not be a routine part of a local authority's assessment of unaccompanied or trafficked children.*"

5.10 "*Child*" is defined in the first sub-paragraph of paragraph 8 of the Statutory Guidance:

> "*Child: anyone who has not yet reached their 18th birthday. 'Children' therefore means 'children and young people under the age of 18' throughout this guidance. Note that, where the person's age is in doubt, they must be treated as a child unless, and until, a case-law compliant age assessment shows the person to be an adult.*"

Age Assessments: legal requirements

5.11 Many asylum seekers arrive in the UK without documentary evidence of their age, or with documentary evidence which is not regarded as reliable. Age determines whether the asylum seeker falls to be accommodated by the Home Office (under s.95 of the Immigration and Asylum Act 1999) or by a local authority under s.20 Children Act 1989.

5.12 An age assessment may be necessary to determine whether a putative child is in fact a child. If age is not clear, an assessment is needed, as stated in B v Merton[15] para. 37. The key case on the procedural requirements for, and content of, an age assessment is *R (B) v London Borough of Merton* [2003] 4 All ER 280, in which Stanley Burton J set out detailed guidance on the process to be followed by local authorities when assessing age, and which has been repeatedly endorsed in subsequent cases.

5.13 In that case, it was held that in cases where it was very obvious that a person was under or over 18 there would normally be no need for prolonged inquiry. However, where the applicant was approaching 18 or was only a few years over 18, but could not provide any reliable documentary evidence to support his or her claim to be a minor, the determination of age could not be made on the basis of appearance only, as it depended on the credibility of the history given, physical appearance and behaviour, and required an assessment of all relevant factors. The decision-maker had to seek to elicit the general background of the applicant, including his family circumstances, his educational background and his history during the previous few years. Ethnic and cultural material might be important. If there was reason to doubt the applicant's statement as to his age, the decision maker would have to make an assessment of his credibility.

5.14 In *R (FZ) v Croydon LBC* [2011] EWCA Civ 59, the Court of Appeal described the decision in *Merton* in the following terms:

> *"3. In R (B) v Merton London Borough Council [2003] EWHC 1689 (Admin), [2003] 4 All ER 280 Stanley Burton J gave guidance in judicial review proceedings on appropriate processes to be adopted where a local authority is assessing a young person's age in borderline cases. The assessment does not require anything approaching a trial and judicialisation of the process it to be avoided. The matter can be determined informally provided there are minimum standards of inquiry and fairness (…). This decision and its guidance have led to the development of what is sometimes referred to as a 'Merton compliant' interview or process."*

15 [2003] EWHC 1689 (Admin)

5.15 The High Court in *VS v The Home Office* [2014] EWHC 2483 QB[16] summarised the relevant legal requirements of an Age Assessment as follows at para. 78 (emphasis added):

> "(1) *The purpose of an age assessment is to establish the chronological age of a young person.*
>
> (2) ***The decision makers cannot determine age solely on the basis of the appearance of the applicant, except in clear cases:*** *Merton per Stanley Burnton at [37].*
>
> (3) ***Physical appearance is a notoriously unreliable basis for assessment of chronological age:*** *NA v LB of Croydon [2009] EWHC 2357 (Admin) per Blake J at [27].*
>
> (4) ***Demeanour can also be notoriously unreliable and by itself constitutes only "somewhat fragile material":*** *NA per Blake J at [28]. Demeanour will generally need to be viewed together with other things. As Collins J stated in A and WK v London Borough of Croydon & Others [2009] EWHC 939 (Admin) at [56]:*
>
>> *"... What is meant by the observation that he appeared to be comfortable in his body? It is difficult to follow what this does mean and how a discomfort with a changing body can manifest itself. Nonetheless, the assessment of his physical appearance and demeanour coupled with the discrepancies and inconsistencies in his account of how he knew his age could justify the conclusion reached."*
>
> (5) ***There should be "no predisposition, divorced from the information and evidence available to the local authority, to assume that an applicant is an adult, or conversely that he is a child":*** *see Merton per Stanley*

16 Upheld by the Court of Appeal: [2015] EWCA Civ 1142

Burnton at [37– 38]. The decision, therefore, needs to be based on particular facts concerning the particular person.

(6) ***There is no burden of proof imposed on the applicant to have to prove his or her age in the course of the assessment:*** *see Merton per Stanley Burnton at [38]. This is confirmed also by R (CJ) v Cardiff CC [2011] EWCA Civ 1590, in which, at [21], Pitchford LJ said this:*

> *"It seems to me that once the court is invited to make a decision upon jurisdictional fact it can do no more than apply the balance of probability to the issue without resorting to the concept of discharge of a burden of proof. In my view, a distinction needs to be made between a legal burden of proof, on the one hand, and the sympathetic assessment of evidence on the other. I accept that in evaluating the evidence it may well be inappropriate to expect from the claimant conclusive evidence of age in circumstances in which he has arrived unattended and without original identity documents. The nature of the evaluation of evidence will depend upon the particular facts of the case."*

(7) *In similar vein,* ***benefit of any doubt is always given to the unaccompanied asylum-seeking child*** *since it is recognised that age assessment is not a scientific process: see A and WK per Collins J at [40].*

(8) *The two social workers who carry out the age assessment should be properly trained and experienced: A and WK per Collins J at [38].*

(9) *The applicant should have an appropriate adult, and should be informed of the right to have one with the purpose of having an appropriate adult also being explained to the applicant: see FZ per Sir Anthony May*

P at [23–25]; J per Coulson J at [14]; and AAM per Lang J at [94(a)].

(10) *The child should be told the purpose of the assessment: see FZ per Sir Anthony May P at [3] (summarising Merton).*

(11) *The decision "must be based on firm grounds and reasons" for it "must be fully set out and explained to the applicant": A and WK per Collins J at [12].*

(12) *The approach of the assessors must involve trying "to establish a rapport with the applicant and any questioning, while recognising the possibility of coaching, should be by means of open-ended and not leading questions". It is "equally important for the assessors to be aware of the customs and practices and any particular difficulties faced by the applicant in his home society": A and WK per Collins J at [13].*

(13) *It is "axiomatic that an applicant should be given a fair and proper opportunity, at a stage when a possible adverse decision is no more than provisional, to deal with important points adverse to his age case which may weigh against him": FZ per Sir Anthony May P at [21]. It is not sufficient that the interviewing social workers withdraw to consider their decision, and then return to present the applicant "with their conclusions without first giving him the opportunity to deal with the adverse points": [22]. See also J per Coulson J at [15]; AAM per Lang J at [94(c)]; and Durani per Coulson at [84–87] (in particular, at [84]: "Elementary fairness requires that the crucial points which are thought to be decisive against an applicant should be identified, in case the applicant has an explanation for them").*

(14) *Assessments devoid of details and/or reasons for the conclusion are not compliant with the Merton guidelines; and the conclusions must be "expressed with sufficient*

> *detail to explain all the main adverse points which the fuller document showed had influenced the decision" (FZ per Sir Anthony May at [22])."*

5.16 The court in *FZ* confirmed that the safeguards should involve what is referred to as a "*minded to*" process during which the young person should be able to comment on any issues potentially adverse to him at the stage where the social workers' decision is no more than provisional [21].

5.17 HHJ Anthony Thornton QC in *AS v London Borough of Croydon* [2011] EWHC 2091 (Admin) [19] described the above procedural safeguards as "*minimum standards*" of fairness.

5.18 In *MVN v LB Greenwich* [2015] EWHC Civ 1942 (Admin) Picken J provided the following guidance as to how best to approach the credibility of a young person:

> *"27. It would, therefore, appear that the primary focus is on the credibility of the person's evidence concerning his or her age, but that it is permissible to have regard to credibility more generally provided that, in looking at credibility more generally, the primary focus to which I have referred is not forgotten. … Miss Luh explained that she accepted that general credibility needs to be factored into the evaluation of the claimant made by the Court, but maintained (rightly, in my view) that there needs nevertheless to be care taken so as to ensure that particular importance is afforded to the credibility of evidence in relation to age.*
>
> *28. Miss Luh identified the following principles drawn from the asylum authorities, which on reflection Miss Screeche-Powell was inclined to recognise were useful also in the context of an age assessment case such as the present:*
>
> *(1) Decision makers considering asylum claims should take everything material into account. Their sources of information will frequently go well beyond the testimony of the applicant and*

include in-country reports and expert testimony: ***Karanakaran v Secretary of State of the Home Department*** *[2000] EWCA Civ 11 per Sedley LJ in his judgment at [2].*

(2) It is an error of law for a decision maker to seek to assess the credibility of a claim in isolation without considering other relevant evidence such as reports regarding a country that corroborate a person's claims: ***R v Immigration Appeal Tribunal ex p Ahmed*** *[1999] INLR 473.*

(3) It is also an error of law to fail to take account of relevant expert evidence when assessing credibility: ***Mibanga v Secretary of State for the Home Department*** *[2005] EWCA Civ 367.*

(4) Further, in assessing credibility in the context of trafficking, this must be done "in the round": ***R (AA (Iraq)) v Secretary of State for the Home Department*** *[2012] EWCA Civ 23 at [67] per Sir David Keene.*

(5) Allowances should be given to the fact that asylum seekers (and similarly victims of trafficking) may have problems giving coherent accounts of their history: ***R (N) v Secretary of State for the Home Department*** *[2008] EWHC 1952 (Admin) at [25] per Blake J ("most people who have experience of obtaining a narrative from asylum seekers from a different language or different culture recognise that time, confidence in the interviewer and the interview process and some patience and some specific direction to pertinent questions is needed to adduce a comprehensive and adequate*

account").

It seems to me that these principles do, indeed, represent useful guidance in the context of an age assessment case.

5.19 In *R(AS) v Croydon* the Court noted that the age assessment process should be undertaken in a non-adversarial, fair, non-stressful and informal manner [19(3)].

5.20 In *R(Q) v Leicestershire County Council, Secretary of State for the Home Department* [2016] EWHC 2087 (Admin) Sir Stephen Silber J. held that:

> "6. *The appropriate approach to assessing age is that:*
>
> a) *Whilst social workers will, in the course of an age assessment, " be able to judge a putative child's general appearance and demeanour, and to make a general credibility judgment from the manner in which he answered their questions. It does not follow that the court would be bound to make the same judgments ." (per Sir Anthony May P giving the judgment of the Court of Appeal in FZ v Croydon, [2011] EWCA Civ 59 at [29] with emphasis added).*
>
> b) *"It would, therefore, appear that the primary focus is on the credibility of the person's evidence concerning his or her age, but that it is permissible to have regard to credibility more generally provided that, in looking at credibility more generally, the primary focus to which I have referred is not forgotten " (per Picken J in R (MVN) v London Borough of Greenwich [2015] EWHC 1942 (Admin) at [27]).*
>
> c) *Decision makers considering asylum claims should take everything material into account. Their sources of information will frequently go well beyond the testimony of the applicant and*

include in-country reports and expert testimony: Karanakaran v Secretary of State of the Home Department [2000] EWCA Civ.11 per Sedley LJ [2].

d) *It is an error of law for a decision maker dealing with asylum claims to seek to assess the credibility of a claimant in isolation without considering other relevant evidence such as reports regarding a country that corroborate a person's claim: R v Immigration Appeal Tribunal ex p Ahmed [1999] INLR 473 .*

e) *It is also an error of law for a decision maker dealing with asylum claims to fail to take account of relevant expert evidence when assessing credibility: Mibanga v Secretary of State for the Home Department [2005] EWCA Cave 367.*

f) *Allowances should be given to the fact that asylum seekers (and similarly victims of trafficking) may have problems giving coherent accounts of their history: R (N) v Secretary of State for the Home Department [2008] EWHC 1952 (Admin) at [25] per Blake J (" most people who have experience of obtaining a narrative from asylum seekers from a different language or different culture recognise that time, confidence in the interviewer and the interview process and some patience and some specific direction to pertinent questions is needed to adduce a comprehensive and adequate account").*

g) *"No margin of discretion is enjoyed by the local authority on this issue" per Lord Hope of Craighead in R (A) v Croydon London Borough Council (supra) [54].*

> 7. *Picken J in R (MVN) (supra) [28] regarded those matters set out in sub-paragraphs (c) to (f) of the last paragraph as "useful guidance in the context of an age assessment case". I respectfully agree.*
>
> 8. *In the present application, neither the Claimant nor the Defendant has the burden of proving the age. In R (CJ) v Cardiff CC (supra) [21], the Court of Appeal made it clear (with emphasis added) that there is no formal "benefit of the doubt" principle and the Court "in evaluating the evidence it may well be inappropriate to expect from the Claimant conclusive evidence of age in circumstances in which he has arrived unattended and without original identity documents. The nature of the evaluation of evidence will depend upon the particular facts of the case."*"

The role of the Court in challenges to local authority age assessments

5.21 In *R(A) v Croydon London Borough Council* the Supreme Court unanimously held that where, following an assessment of a young person's age, there remains a dispute between that person and the local authority concerned, it is for the Court to determine the young person's age as a matter of fact. Baroness Hale held that:

> *"27 (...) the question whether a person is a child is a different kind of question. There is a right or wrong answer. It may be difficult to determine what that answer is. The decision-makers may have to do their best on the basis of less than perfect or conclusive evidence. But that is true of many questions of fact which regularly come before the courts. That does not prevent them from being questions for the courts rather than for other kinds of decision makers."*

5.22 The supervisory role of the court means that neither party has the burden of proof in respect of its case: *R (CJ) v Cardiff City Council* [2011] EWCA Civ 1590. The Court must adopt an "*inquisitorial role*" to determine "*whether the precedent fact existed on the balance of probabilities* (*R (CJ)* [22]). The Court's decision *"will, in the case of disputed evidence, be decided following appropriate discovery and cross- examination"*: AS [21].

Assessing a young person's account vis-à-vis the local authority's age assessment

5.23 In *R (AS) v Croydon* [2011] at [21], HHJ Anthony Thornton QC described the correct approach to be taken by the Court in age assessment disputes (emphasis added):

> *"The Administrative Court's decision must be reached on the balance of probabilities and will, in the case of disputed evidence, be decided following appropriate discovery and cross-examination.* ***The assessment or assessments being challenged are evidence which should be taken into account with all other evidence and age assessments adduced at the hearing*** *(...)."*

5.24 In *A*, Lord Hope, in his concurring judgment [54] confirmed that the Court should afford "*no margin of discretion*" to the local authority's own view of an individual's age; it does not carry more weight than the young person's account as to their age. Where a fact-finding hearing takes place in a disputed age case, the role of the Court is to evaluate all the available evidence and it is not constrained to agree with one party or another as to the disputed issue of age, but is required to determine age i.e. to ascribe a date of birth to the applicant which can then be set out by way of a declaratory provision of an order.

Local Authority duties to a LAC

5.25 By s.22 of the Act a child accommodated by a local authority under s.20 for more than 24 hours becomes a "looked after" child and the local authority has duties to safeguard and promote the child's welfare, including to promote their educational achievement, and to make use of services available for children cared for by their own parents as appears reasonable to the local authority.

5.26 Section 22C of the Children Act 1989 makes provision for the ways in which looked after children are to be accommodated and maintained. A looked after child can live with a parent, a person with parental responsibility for them, a person named in a child arrangements order, or a foster parent, or in a children's home, or be placed in accordance with "other arrangements" – s. 22C(6)(d).

5.27 Section 11(2)(a) of the Children Act 2004 provides:

> Each person and body to whom this section applies must make arrangements for ensuring that–
>
> (a) their functions are discharged having regard to the need to safeguard and promote the welfare of children;

Duties to a care leaver

5.28 Sections 23A-23C CA 1989 contain the leaving care duties. Those duties are owed to an "eligible child", "a relevant child", or a "former relevant child" as defined. It is these duties, to an over-18, which are within the prohibited forms of support and assistance specified at para.1 of Schedule 3 to the NIAA 2002. A child "looked after" as an unaccompanied asylum seeker is potentially entitled to support as a care leaver post-18 (but subject to the application of Schedule 3).

5.29 An "eligible child" is, pursuant to paragraph 19B(2) of Schedule 2 to the 1989 and regulation 40 of the Care Planning, Placement and Case Review (England) Regulations 2010/959 ("the 2010 Regulations"), a child who (a) is aged 16 or 17, and (b) has been looked after by a local authority for a period of (or periods amounting to) 13 weeks, which began after he reached the age of 14 and ended after he reached the age of sixteen.

5.30 The 2010 Regulations define the *"responsible authority"* as being the authority *"that looks after"* the child.

5.28 A "relevant child" is, pursuant to section 23A(2), a child who (a) is not being looked after by any local authority, (b) was, before last ceasing to be looked after, an "eligible child", and (c) is aged 16 or 17.

5.29 A "former relevant child" is defined by section 23C (1) of the CA 1989 as follows:

(1) Each local authority shall have the duties provided for in this section towards—

(a) a person who has been a relevant child for the purposes of section 23A (and would be if he were under eighteen), and in relation to whom they were the last responsible authority; and

(b) a person who was being looked after by them when he attained the age of eighteen, and immediately before ceasing to be looked after was an eligible child,

and in this section such a person is referred to as a "former relevant child".

Statutory guidance

5.30 The Department for Education has produced statutory guidance entitled "Care of unaccompanied migrant children and child victims of modern slavery". It is dated November 2017 and is described as "*Statutory guidance for [local authorities] and professionals who support unaccompanied migrant children, who may be victims, or potential victims, of modern slavery.*"

5.31 This guidance provides in relation to "age determination":

> 35. Many unaccompanied and trafficked children arrive in the UK without documentation or with forged or counterfeit documents. Where the age of a person is uncertain and there are reasons to believe they are a child, that person is presumed to be a child in order to receive immediate access to assistance, support and protection in accordance with section 51 of the Modern Slavery Act 2015 . Where an age assessment is required, local authorities must adhere to standards established within case law. Age assessments should only be carried out where there is reason to doubt that the individual is the age they claim. Age assessments should not be a routine part of a local authority's assessment

of unaccompanied or trafficked children. Further advice and practice guidance can be found in the *Age Assessment Guidance,* published by the Association of Directors of Children's Services (ADCS) in October 2015. It is also important to note that an ADCS – Home Office information sharing protocol has been produced.

Non-statutory guidance

ADCS Guidance

5.32 The Association of Directors of Children's Services ("ADCS"), the leadership association for statutory directors of children's services, produced guidance in October 2015 entitled "Age Assessment Guidance". It is not statutory guidance but has nonetheless been relied upon by courts as highly persuasive: in *R (S) v London Borough of Croydon* [2017] EWHC 265 (Admin), its authors were noted to have "considerable expertise in their field" [41] so and it will be relevant, at least, to any question of whether departures from the statutory guidance are justified [50]. In practice, the ADCS Guidance is relevant to age disputes which come before the courts.

Procedural requirements

5.33 These include ensuring that there is a suitable interpreter and appropriate adult. The assessment should be conducted by two suitably qualified social workers. Account should be taken of any physical or mental health needs of the putative child. Matters regarded as potentially adverse to the applicant should be put to him for comment, and there should be a "minded to" procedure so that the provisional decision is communicated at a time when there is still an opportunity for comment to be made capable of influencing the outcome.

Accommodation pending age assessment

5.34 In terms of accommodation pending assessment, it was held in in *R(S) v Croydon* [2017] EWHC 265 (Admin) that an applicant is to be treated as a child unless or until a case-law compliant age assessment concludes that they are an adult.

5.35 The ADCS guidance states that:

> Other than in exceptional circumstances, children and young people will be looked after under Section 20 of the Children Act 1989 whilst the age assessment process continues.

The same guidance states that bed and breakfast accommodation is not suitable.

5.36 The question of "exceptional circumstances" was considered by the High Court in *AB & Ors, R (On the Application Of) v London Borough of Brent* [2021] EWHC 2843. In that case asylum seekers placed by the Home Office in adult accommodation (in a hotel) claimed to be children and sought assistance from Brent, in whose area the hotel was located, under the Children Act 1989. It was held that the timescales for an assessment of their age did not amount to the sort of exceptional circumstances which might justify a putative child not being looked after under s.20 pending assessment, and that Brent's decision that the putative children should remain accommodated in hotel accommodation with adult asylum seekers pending age assessment was unlawful.

Challenging an age assessment

5.37 An applicant who is dissatisfied with the determination is entitled to challenge it by way of judicial review, however the type of judicial review involves the court conducting a fact-finding hearing (see *R(A) v LB Croydon* [2009] UKSC 8) and making the determination itself, in line with the Merton criteria, as to the applicant's age. This fact finding takes place if the applicant is able to overcome the permission threshold set out in *R(FZ) v LB Croydon* [para.9]. That permission threshold is a low one: it requires the court to take a claimant's case "at its highest" and decide whether it could succeed at trial on that basis.

5.38 In practical terms, such fact-finding is generally transferred to the Upper Tribunal once permission has been granted. Under changes contained within Part 4 of the Nationality and Borders Bill, a putative child seeking to challenge an age assessment will have a statutory right of appeal to the First Tier tribunal, thereby bypassing the need to issue a claim for judicial review and to have the permission threshold determined.

The "short form" age assessment

When is a full age assessment required?

5.39 B v Merton makes clear that in a clear or obvious case, an assessment may not be required. In *R (K) v Milton Keynes Council* [2019] EWHC 1723 (Admin) the local authority determined that there was no need for a full age assessment: the view of its social workers was that it was so obvious on the basis of appearance that the applicant was over 18 as to be unnecessary to undertake a detailed age assessment. An application for judicial review and for interim relief was made, and interim relief was refused on the basis that *Merton* recognised that no full assessment was required in clear cases, but was needed only if there was doubt.

5.40 In R *(AB) v Kent County Council* [2020] EWHC 109 (Admin) there had been a short form age assessment of an asylum seeker who claimed to be 15 but who Kent considered to be between 20 and 25 on the basis of appearance and demeanour. It was held that it was legitimate for a local authority to assess age based on an abbreviated assessment of physical appearance and demeanour, but in making such an assessment the authority must take "...into account the margin for error in the abbreviated nature of the assessment." No guidance was given as to what that margin should be as it "may depend on the circumstances of the assessment".

5.41 Home Office guidance issued for the use of Home Office caseworkers "*Assessing Age*"[17] dated 14 January 2022 states that:

The policy is specifically designed to allow **a large margin of error in favour of the claimant's claim to be a child.** It achieves this by requiring Home Office staff to only treat them as an adult on the basis of their

---

[17] https://assets.publishing.service.gov.uk/government/uploads/system/uploads/attachment_data/file/1045849/Assessing_age.pdf

physical appearance and demeanour, where they conclude that these indicators **very strongly suggest they are significantly over 18 years of age**. This takes account of the challenges in assessing a claimant's age in such circumstances. [emphasis added]

5.42 *R(MA) v Secretary of State for the Home Department* [2022] EWHC 98 (Admin) was a challenge to the lawfulness of detention by the Home Office and in connection with the lawfulness of that detention, to guidance issued to social workers at a Home Office facility, the Kent Intake Unit. The age assessments were conducted on day of the applicants' arrival in the UK. They did not have an independent appropriate adult and there was no follow up for the purposes of clarification, correction or further information. The interviews took an hour or less and upon it being concluded that the applicants were over 18, they were transferred to an Immigration Removal Centre for three and five days before being placed in adult asylum support accommodation in Coventry.

The Court recognised that detention for the purpose of a short formalised process, within the overall parameters of the duration of Schedule 2 paragraph 16(1) of the Immigration Act 1971, would not be unlawful provided it was in conjunction with a *Merton* compliant age assessment. Conversely, the Court considered that any prolongation of detention for the purpose of an initial assessment which was not *Merton* compliant was unlawful.

The guidance to Kent Intake Unit social workers was found to be unlawful, because to assess age in a non-obvious case where the applicant has just arrived in the UK and had been detained and was without the support of an appropriate adult, was not *Merton* compliant. It should be emphasised that the court was concerned with cases where it was not obvious that the individual was over 18 i.e. this was not the sort of clear and obvious situation where a *Merton* assessment would not be required. The Home Office guidance which was challenged in this case was withdrawn in January 2022.

Key Points

- In a clear case, where a sufficient margin for error has been allowed, it may not be necessary to conduct a full *Merton* compliant age assessment

- Where there is doubt, a *Merton* compliant age assessment should be conducted

- Except in exceptional circumstances, a putative child should be accommodated in line with s.20 CA 1989 pending assessment

- The ADCS guidance contains helpful practical guidance on assessments, including as to the procedural requirements for an assessment to be lawful

- Where an age assessment is challenged, it will be for a court to decide the applicant's age, having considered all the evidence, including post-assessment material. This may include oral evidence from, and cross examination of, the applicant and the assessing social workers.

CHAPTER SIX

HUMAN RIGHTS ASSESSMENT

6.1 Para.3 of Schedule 3 NIAA 2002 provides for an exception to the prohibition on the forms of support and assistance specified in para.1 *if, and to the extent that, the provision of support is necessary to prevent a breach of a person's human rights.*

6.2 While there is no specified or prescribed form for such an assessment, there are a number of key issues that should be addressed either within the human rights assessment or by way of a separate assessment.

6.3 General points on human rights assessment for Schedule 3 purposes:

(a) the assessment is of breach of a *person's* human rights and therefore may require consideration of *persons other than the applicant*[18];

(b) all ECHR rights are potentially relevant to this assessment, however the provisions most likely to require close consideration are articles 3 and 8 ECHR;

(c) Article 3 is an absolute right, whereas article 8 is qualified. That means that there are no circumstances in which interference with article 3 ECHR would be lawful, but in relation to article 8, interference may be lawful if it meets certain condition;

(d) For article 3 purposes, the core issue on a human rights assessment is whether remaining in the UK without support would amount to inhuman or degrading treatment;

(e) Issues relating to an article 3 breach in country of origin (if the proposal is for the applicant to relocate there) can and should be

18 *R(M) v LB Islington* [2004] EWCA Civ 235 para.46

the subject of a claim for asylum (see the definition of a claim for asylum in s.94 of the Immigration and Asylum Act 1999, which includes a claim under art.3 ECHR).

Article 3 ECHR

> "No one shall be subjected to torture or to inhuman or degrading treatment or punishment"

6.4 It is "inhuman or degrading treatment" which is relevant in the context of a human rights assessment where the availability of support is in issue.

6.5 *R (Limbuela) v Secretary of State for the Home Department* [2006] 1 AC 396 arose from a decision by the Home Office that asylum applicants who had not claimed asylum as soon as practicable would not be entitled to Home Office support while their asylum claims were considered. This was notwithstanding the condition of "destitution" being met by reason of homelessness, lack of access to food and being subject to a prohibition on seeking employment. The issue was whether the removal of support amounted to a breach of article 3 ECHR. The House of Lords considered that there was such a breach, and in doing so gave guidance, in the context of support for asylum seekers, on the circumstances in which a breach of Article 3 ECHR might arise. Lord Hope, at [54] said:

> But the European Court has all along recognised that ill-treatment must attain a minimum level of severity if it is to fall within the scope of the expression "inhuman or degrading treatment or punishment": *Ireland v United Kingdom* (1978) 2 EHRR 25, 80, para 167; *A v United Kingdom* (1998) 27 EHRR 611, 629, para 20; *V v United Kingdom* (1999) 30 EHRR 121, para 71. In *Pretty v United Kingdom* 35 EHRR 1, 33, para 52, the court said: "As regards the types of 'treatment' which fall within the scope of article 3 of the Convention, the court's case law refers to 'ill-treatment' that attains a minimum level of severity and involves actual bodily injury or intense physical or mental suffering. Where treatment humiliates or debases an individual showing a lack of respect for, or diminishing, his

> or her human dignity or arouses feelings of fear, anguish or inferiority capable of breaking an individual's moral and physical resistance, it may be characterised as degrading and also fall within the prohibition of article 3. The suffering which flows from naturally occurring illness, physical or mental, may be covered by article 3, where it is, or risks being, exacerbated by treatment, whether flowing from conditions of detention, expulsion or other measures, for which the authorities can be held responsible. It has also said that the assessment of this minimum is relative, as it depends on all the circumstances of the case such as the nature and context of the treatment or punishment that is in issue. The fact is that it is impossible by a simple definition to embrace all human conditions that will engage article 3."

6.6 It should be noted that *Limbuela* does not give rise to a "freestanding" article 3 based claim for state support. The case was solely concerned with the construction of s.55(5)(a) of the NIAA 2002, as made clear in paragraphs 1 and 7 of Lord Bingham's judgment. So while the case is instructive in terms of the criteria by which a breach of article 3 on account of removal of support is to be assessed, it is not authority for a general article 3 right to support.

6.7 It will be a question of fact to be assessed as to whether an applicant would experience homelessness and destitution amounting to inhuman and degrading treatment if not provided with a prohibited form of local authority support. In some cases, the factual conclusion may be that a breach of article 3 can be avoided by support from family, friends, charitable organisations etc. Such inquiry is likely to take place in particular where there has been support provided to the applicant (other than by the state) which is now reported to have ceased. In *R(O) v LB Lambeth* [2016] EWHC 937 (Admin) the context was an assessment of whether a child was "in need" for the purposes of s.17 Children Act 1989. However the conclusion is equally applicable to the factual inquiry about destitution and homelessness for article 3 purposes:

6.8 If the applicant for assistance does not provide adequate contact details for family and friends who have provided assistance in the past, or cannot provide a satisfactory explanation as to why the sources of support which existed in the past have ceased to exist, the local authority may reasonably conclude that it is not satisfied that the family is homeless or destitute, so that no power to provide arises [19]

Article 3 and the "minimum level of severity"

6.9 In *D v. United Kingdom* (1997) 24 EHRR the applicant was a native of St Kitts, who had never lived in the UK but was caught with a substantial amount of cocaine on his arrival at Heathrow. He pleaded guilty to importation and was sentenced to 6 years imprisonment. Upon his release three years later he was detained pending deportation. Whilst in prison he was diagnosed with HIV and sought to resist deportation as a result. His immune system was severally compromised.

6.10 In June 1996 D's life expectancy was said to be 8-12 months. He was however still being treated with drugs [15]. At the time of hearing in February 1997 his prognosis was uncertain but his counsel stated that his life was drawing to a close "as the experts had predicted" [21]. D's CD4 count was below 10 and he suffered from continuing chest infections, malaise, skin rashes and weight loss. Limited hospital care was available in St Kitts. D had no family or friends there that would care for him. No social provision would be available in St Kitts.

The ECtHR concluded that to deport D would constitute a breach of Article 3.

6.11 In *BB v. France* (as summarised in *N v. UK* para 35 at D68) the applicant's HIV had reached an advanced stage, requiring repeated hospital stays, but had stabilised as a result of antiretroviral treatment which he claimed would not be available to him in his home country, the Democratic Republic of the Congo. The Commission concluded that it would be violation of Article 3 to deport him, holding that "*To expect him to confront his illness alone, without any support from family members, was likely to make it impossible for him to maintain human dignity as the disease ran its course.*" The case was referred to the Court but a settlement was reached before the hearing.

6.12 *Paposhvili v Belgium* (App No. 41738/10), [2017] Imm AR 876 concerned a Georgian national who had been living in Belgium and who had been sentenced to three years' imprisonment.

While in prison, diagnosis was made of chronic lymphocytic leukaemia: this was reported to be life-threatening and to result in a life expectancy between three and five years. Other medical conditions included hepatitis C and pulmonary tuberculosis, and a stroke, resulting in permanent paralysis of the left arm. Applications for leave to remain were refused by the Belgian state.

The Grand Chamber of the EctHR considered the case after the Applicant's death, because of "special circumstances".

Its judgment addresses the "very exceptional circumstances" in which it would find a breach of article 3 in removal cases of seriously ill persons, laid down in the earlier authorities of *D v UK* (1997) 24 EHRR 423 and *N v UK* (2008) 47 EHRR 885 [GC].

The Court in *Paposhvilli* rowed back somewhat from the previously restrictive approach by holding, at paragraph 183, that the very exceptional cases referred to in *N*:

> "*...refer to situations involving the removal of a seriously ill person in which substantial grounds have been shown for believing that he or she, although not at imminent risk of dying, would face a real risk, on account of the absence of appropriate treatment in the receiving country or the lack of access to such treatment, of being exposed to a serious, rapid and irreversible decline in his or her state of health resulting in intense suffering or to a significant reduction in life expectancy.*"

The "high threshold" for article 3 was maintained, but a distinction drawn between end of life cases and those which are not end of life, and would need to be "very exceptional" for the purpose of article 3, in particular, where there is a risk of a decline which either results in "intense suffering" or a "significant reduction in life expectancy". The State is expected to assess whether the applicant would have access to care and medical facilities in the destination country, (including the ability to access such care by reference to cost), and social and family networks.

There remains no right to specific treatment in the receiving state; and a mere disparity between health-care systems is not, in itself, sufficient to engage article 3. The question remains whether the act of removal will expose the applicant to a violation of article 3, according to the "real risk" test set out at para.183 of the Court's judgment.

6.13 In *AM (Zimbabwe)* [2020] UKSC 17, the Supreme Court held that the appropriate Article 3 medical threshold is that held to apply in *Paposhvili*.

AM (Zimbabwe) sets out the two elements to determining an Article 3 medical claim: a) the substantive test (as per *Paposhvili*) and b) the procedural obligations.

Article 8 ECHR

> "1 Everyone has the right to respect for his private and family life, his home and his correspondence.
>
> 2 There shall be no interference by a public authority with the exercise of this right except such as is in accordance with the law and is necessary in a democratic society in the interests of national security, public safety or the economic well being of the country, for the prevention of disorder or crime, for the protection of health or morals, or for the protection of the rights and freedoms of others".

6.14 Article 8 has been held to be capable of imposing positive obligations on the State as well as negative obligations to refrain from the specified interference: see *Marckx v Belgium* [**1979**] ECHR 2:

> *'the object of the Article [8] is "essentially" that of protecting the individual against arbitrary interference by the public authorities. Nevertheless it does not merely compel the State to*

> *abstain from such interference: in addition to this primarily negative undertaking, there may be positive obligations inherent in an effective "respect" for family life...*

6.15 However, such positive obligations will be more sparingly imposed where they involve an allocation of scarce resources, in which case a "margin of appreciation" is applied, the effect of which may be to confer a requirement that there be deference to the State to determine where and how it allocates its resources, as discussed by the Supreme Court in *McDonald v RB Kensington and Chelsea* [2011] UKSC 33 at [16].

6.17 Interference with article 8 is permissible, but only where the interference is *necessary* in relation to one of the specified national interests. Economic well-being would potentially justify interference where the issue is one of allocation of scarce local authority resources. However, such interference must also be *proportionate*. The human rights assessment and/ or decision must engage with the type of interference, the extent of the interference, and assess whether this is proportionate.

6.18 Where children are involved there are other relevant duties. The first is the duty on a local authority under s.11(2) Children Act 2004 to

> ... make arrangements for ensuring that—
>
> (a) their functions are discharged having regard to the need to safeguard and promote the welfare of children; ...

6.19 The second is the obligation, set out in *ZH (Tanzania) v Secretary of State* [2011] UKSC 4 to identify the best interests of the child, and then in conducting the proportionality balancing exercise, to ensure that those interests are a "primary consideration". This means that they must be considered first, and then consideration given to whether those interests can be outweighed by the cumulative effect of other relevant matters. The case also stands as authority for the proposition that the child's own views as to where his best interests lie should be identified and taken into account, in some cases by consulting the child themselves " who wishes to express a view and is old enough to do so". It is noted that the child's best interests may not align with those of the parent [34 –7].

Relocation to country of origin

6.20 Assessment of article 8 ECHR in the context of persons from abroad arises most frequently in the situation of an applicant who is considered to be able to leave the UK and relocate (usually to country of origin) and by doing so, avoid the state of destitution and homelessness which would result if the applicant remained in the UK without accommodation or support. Such relocation inevitably engages article 8 because the applicant will likely have an established family and / or private life in the UK.

6.21 A local authority cannot compel the relocation from the UK of an applicant. It has no removal powers (in contrast to the Home Office). However it can:

(a) determine in an appropriate case that an applicant is able to relocate abroad, or

(b) that support can be provided to enable relocation, and

(c) either provide support itself, or

(d) offer signposting to the Home Office voluntary returns programme (which offers practical support as well as financial assistance)[19] or to embassies of the country of proposed return which may be able to assist with repatriation.

6.22 In *R(Kimani) v LB Lambeth* [2003] EWCA Civ 1150, [2004] 1 WLR 272 the applicant was an ineligible person as defined by Schedule 3 NIAA 2002. She had sought leave to remain which had been refused, and was pursuing an appeal against that decision which the Court of Appeal described as "clearly specious". Lambeth's decision in relation to support for her and her child under the Children Act 1989 was to find her ineligible, and to conclude that it was not necessary to provide such

[19] https://www.gov.uk/return-home-voluntarily

support in order to prevent a breach of ECHR rights because she had the option to relocate, with her son, to Kenya. The Court of Appeal upheld Lambeth's decision, stating that:

> 6.23 We do not consider that either Article 3 or Article 8 imposes a duty on the State to provide the appellant with support. She has not been granted leave to enter or remain in this country... no infringement of Article 8 would result from requiring her to return to her own country pending the determination of her appeal. There is no impediment to her returning to her own country. A State owes no duty under the Convention to provide support to foreign nationals who are permitted to enter their territory but who are in a position freely to return home. [49]

When is relocation abroad not an option?

6.24 A human rights assessment must take account of the individual circumstances of the applicant which may be relevant to whether, in practical terms, the applicant is able to relocate abroad. Relevant matters are suggested to include

(a) whether there is a safe route of travel (including any government advice in relation to travel, and in particular whether that advice applies to nationals of the country in question or to foreigners);

(b) whether any health condition precludes travel (an example might be medical advice against flying in late pregnancy);

(c) documentation to travel (this may be a temporary issue only, and capable of resolution, for example by seeking assistance from the voluntary returns programme);

(d) whether all family members whose travel is proposed are able to relocate together to the proposed destination. This may require consideration of citizenship and visa issues potentially requiring specialist advice.

Clue v Birmingham: a legal bar to relocation as an available means of avoiding a human rights breach

6.25 Availability of relocation abroad is not just a question of factual inquiry as to the applicant's circumstances. It also requires consideration of whether as a matter of law relocation is an available option.

6.26 *Clue v Birmingham [*2010] EWCA Civ 460 concerned an applicant who sought support for herself and her children under s.17 Children Act 1989. At the time of application to Birmingham, she had an application pending with the Home Office for indefinite leave to remain. Birmingham decided that it would not exercise its power under s.17 to provide support and accommodation as it considered that the family was able to return to Jamaica where they could continue to enjoy a family life. In light of that, Birmingham determined that a refusal to provide support and accommodation would not breach their rights under article 8 ECHR. It was identified that the family required assistance to enable them to travel to Jamaica and possibly also a resettlement grant. That decision was challenged and the challenge succeeded at first instance, following which Birmingham appealed to the Court of Appeal.

6.27 The Court of Appeal considered the case of *Kimani* (see 6.22 above) and found it to be distinguishable from this case, because (i) it was concerned with a claim based on an alleged breach of the right to family life and not private life; and (ii) it was reasonable in that case to require the claimant to return to Kenya and to pursue her pending appeal from there. That was a clear point of distinction because in *Clue*, requiring the family to relocate to Jamaica would have resulted in them losing the right to pursue their application for indefinite leave to remain, as departing from the UK would be regarded as abandonment of the application to the Home Office.

6.28 *Grant v Lambeth* [2004] EWCA Civ 1711, [2005] 1 WLR 1781 was discussed, and found not to be clear authority for any proposition in relation to article 8 because the case had been argued by reference to domestic law principles and not under the ECHR.

6.29 On the key issue, it was held there is a fundamental difference between the social services functions of a local authority and the immigration functions of the Secretary of State, and deciding on the merits of an application for leave to remain is the function of the Secretary of State. The rights protected by the ECHR include, in addition to the substantive rights, the procedural rights necessary to assert those substantive rights, in other words, there is a right to make an application, to have it determined by the appropriate authority, and not to have that process curtailed or pre-determined by a local authority decision on support. At para.63 it is stated that:

> ...in enacting Schedule 3 [NIAA 2002], Parliament cannot reasonably have intended to confer a general power on local authorities to pre-empt the determination by the Secretary of State of applications for leave to remain. In my judgment, **save in hopeless or abusive cases, the duty imposed on local authorities to act so as to avoid a breach of an applicant's Convention rights does not require or entitle them to decide how the Secretary of State will determine an application for leave to remain** or, in effect, determine such an application themselves by making it impossible for the applicant to pursue it. [my emphasis]

6.30 So a local authority, when considering Schedule 3 in the case of an applicant who has a pending application to the Home Office for leave to remain, is limited to assessing whether the immigration application is *hopeless or abusive.*

6.31 That sets a higher threshold than whether the local authority consider the application for leave to remain to be likely to succeed, and a hopeless or abusive case is likely to be one where there have been multiple applications on the same facts, or some misrepresentation amounting to abuse. *R(SB) v LB Camden* [2018] EWHC 2275 (Admin) see 6.37 below is an example of a hopeless or abusive further application for leave to remain, at para.22.

6.32 If the application to the Home Office does not meet the hopeless or abusive threshold, the local authority is not lawfully able to propose that the applicant leaves the UK. In terms of whether it is "necessary" to provide support to avoid a breach of human rights, the local authority may still consider alternative forms of support in the UK.

The reach of *Clue*

6.33 Subsequent to Clue, there has been consideration of what application to the Home Office is capable of giving rise to the procedural human rights protections identified.

In *R(KA) v Essex CC*[20] the Claimant was a failed asylum seeker who had been refused asylum but had not been served with the removal directions which would trigger her being entitled to appeal the refusal. She also intended to make a further application for leave to remain based on new evidence [48(2) & 54] at the date of Essex's decision. By the date of hearing, that further application had been made. The Deputy High Court Judge held at [55-56] that

> Thus I conclude that there was a substantive Convention procedural right comprised in the statutory right to appeal against the immigration decision for removal directions which would be required for the removal of the Claimant and her family in the absence of any other supervening event. It is equally plain in my judgment that the decision to remove support was made in recognition that the consequence would be the return of the Claimant and her family to Nigeria and that in effect that would deprive them of their procedural right of appeal under the 2002 Act against the immigration decision when it was made.
>
> Notwithstanding that clear linkage between the decision to withdraw support and the procedural right, there is scant, if any, consideration of the implications in the Defendant's assessment or as part of its recorded decision. In particular it was not suggested that the potential appeal against an immigration decision would be obviously hopeless or abusive, the response to the protocol letter simply indicating that the authority was unable to assess the strength of any proposed case. In my judgment, the proper approach on the facts of this case, should have been to provide support so far

20 [2013] EWHC 43 (Admin) | **[2013] 1 W.L.R. 1163**

as necessary to preserve that procedural right to protection of the Claimant's and her family's article 8 rights unless the Defendant concluded that it was in effect obviously hopeless or abusive.

6.34 While the extension of *Clue* to the intention to make a further application may be regarded as *obiter* (because by date of hearing the fresh application had been made) it is a factor which was considered to be capable of founding a procedural human right requiring consideration within a human rights assessment.

6.35 However, in *R(MN) v LB Hackney*[21], Leggatt J. (as he then was) expressed doubt as to the correctness of the approach in *KA* and declined to follow it [84], noting that it was, at that time, the subject of a pending appeal.

Essex's appeal to the Court of Appeal was subsequently dismissed[22] as by the date of appeal, the Court of Appeal regarded the appeal as academic.

6.36 In *R(OA) v LB Camden*[23], permission to apply for judicial review was granted having regard to and relying upon *KA* [55].

6.37 In *R(SB) v LB Camden* [2018] EWHC 2275 (Admin) there was no pending application for leave to remain, but an appointment had been made with the Home Office to make further submissions in relation to a previously failed application for such leave. In refusing permission to apply for judicial review this was held not to amount to an outstanding application to the Home Office for leave to remain [21] and, on the facts, even if the intention to make further submissions were a pending application, it was a hopeless or abusive one because it was a repeat application in circumstances where three previous applications had been rejected [22].

---

21 [2013] EWHC 1205 (Admin) | [2013] 5 WLUK 269

22 [2013] EWCA Civ 1261 | [2013] 1 W.L.R. 2882

23 https://www.bailii.org/ew/cases/EWHC/Admin/2019/2537.pdf

Interplay between local authority support, and speed of Home Office decision making

6.38 A practical difficulty arises from the time it can take for immigration applications to be resolved, initially by way of a decision from the Home Office. While applications are pending, an applicant may be supported by a local authority, in line with *Clue of Birmingham CC*, in circumstances where both the applicant and supporting local authority want a swift decision on the application so that the applicant can access work and mainstream welfare support (if permitted) and the local authority can consider whether that addresses the needs of the child it has identified.

6.39 This delay was a relevant factor in the circumstances presented to the Court in *Clue*, to which the Secretary of State for the Home Department responded in terms which are recorded at para.85 of the Court of Appeal's judgment:

> The Secretary of State has summarised his position in the following terms: (i) the CRD [case resolution directorate] will prioritise the consideration of cases involving applicants who are supported by local authorities in the same way as it prioritises the cases of applicants who are supported by the Secretary of State; and (ii) he will review the decision-making processes in the CRD, having regard to the need to safeguard and promote the welfare of children who are in the UK and having regard to his statutory guidance (including para 2.20 thereof, which states that "every effort must....be made to achieve timely decisions for [children]").

6.40 On the basis of this statement of position, it is possible for a local authority and/ or an applicant to seek to expedite decision making where there is a pending application for leave to remain on behalf of an applicant who is in receipt of support from a local authority.

Who decides whether a breach of human rights will occur?

6.41 Initially, it is the local authority which makes this assessment, and the decision as to whether support is necessary to prevent a breach of human rights will be potentially amenable to challenge by way of judicial review on the usual public law grounds.

6.42 However the court which is considering a claim for judicial review, as a public authority for the purposes of the Human Rights Act 1998, is subject to the duty in s.6 of that Act not to act incompatibly with Convention rights and in doing so must also ensure that other public authorities (such as a local authority) do not act incompatibly with Convention rights. This requires a merits based review of whether a breach of human rights will occur, i.e. examination of the alleged breach on a factual basis, which is capable of taking into account materials post-dating the public law decision[24].

"Child in need" in country of origin

Assessment

6.43 Where the service which is being sought is support for a family under s.17 Children Act 1989, a local authority is required to assess the needs of the child in accordance with statutory guidance, "Working Together to Safeguard Children" (2018). As held in *CTM&U v LB Southwark* [2016] EWCA Civ 707; [2016] HLR 36, a child whose needs arise from her family not having recourse to public funds is not to be treated differently to any other child in need, therefore the *Working Together* guidance is the applicable scheme for an assessment of need.

Local Protocols

6.44 Para.45-50 of the *Working Together* guidance requires that a local authority produce a local protocol for assessment. This "should reflect where assessments for some children will require particular care" [para.48]. The groups identified as needing particular care include

24 See *R(de Almeida) v RB Kensington and Chelsea* [2012] EWHC 1082 (Admin) at [74] and [85]

"asylum seeking children, children considered at risk of gang activity... [the latter group is capable of including child victims of trafficking, discussed further below].

The principles of assessment

6.45 The purpose of assessment, according to the statutory guidance, is said to be "...always:

- to gather important information about a child and family
- to analyse their needs and/or the nature and level of any risk and harm being suffered by the child
- to decide whether the child is a child in need (section 17) or is suffering or likely to suffer significant harm (section 47)
- to provide support to address those needs to improve the child's outcomes and welfare and where necessary to make them safe"

High quality assessments are discussed at para.58 and are said to be:

- ...child-centred. Where there is a conflict of interest, decisions should be made in the child's best interests: be rooted in child development: be age-appropriate; and be informed by evidence
- ... focused on action and outcomes for children
- are holistic in approach, addressing the child's needs within their family and any risks the child faces from within the wider community
- ensure equality of opportunity
- involve children, ensuring that their voice is heard and provide appropriate support to enable this where the child has specific communication needs

- involve families
- identify risks to the safety and welfare of children
- build on strengths as well as identifying difficulties
- are integrated in approach
- are multi-agency and multi-disciplinary
- are a continuing process, not an event
- lead to action, including the provision of services
- review services provided on an ongoing basis
- are transparent and open to challenge

6.46 As reflected in para.58, an assessment should lead to action, including service provision. In the case of a family from abroad without recourse to public funds, a potential action might be for the local authority to offer support to the family to relocate to country of origin.

6.47 As this support can be provided only because a child has been identified as being a "child in need" as defined by s.17(10), the local authority must be satisfied that any provision it makes in order to prevent a breach of a person's human rights *meets the identified needs of the child:* see *R(M) v LB Islington* at [49][25].

6.48 Being satisfied that a child's needs will be met abroad may require consideration, in line with the *Working Together* guidance, as to the child's circumstances in the proposed destination in relation to education, health and emotional development as well as the ability of the

[25] "Islington would have to bear three considerations in mind before it could lawfully discharge its Children Act duty by an offer of tickets rather than by providing support, including accommodation, in the United Kingdom. First, it would have to be confident that the child will cease to be "in need" if removed to Guyana…" [49]

child's parent(s) (with or without support) to meet needs for housing and subsistence.

The assessment is required to be child centred, to focus on the best interests of the child, and depending on the child's age and maturity, would need to include the child's wishes and feelings. The guidance emphasises that assessment is a process and not an event, and may need to be reviewed in light of further information coming to light.

Interplay between leaving care provisions under Children Act 1989 and Home Office support for current and failed asylum seekers

6.49 This issue may arise in the context of a human rights assessment consequential to a finding that a former relevant child ("FRC") i.e. a person owed "leaving care" duties is ineligible for assistance by reference to Schedule 3 NIAA 2002.

This would arise only if the FRC is an "ineligible" person, as defined, potentially if he is a failed asylum seeker who is in the UK in breach of the immigration laws (Schedule 3, para.7). The local authority which would owe leaving care duties, in assessing whether a failure to do so would breach the human rights of the FRC, may take into account alternative forms of support available in the UK to the FRC. The question is whether support for a failed asylum seeker (under s.4 Immigration and Asylum Act 1999) is available to a FRC? Such support has been found to be support of last resort – see *Westminster CC v NASS* [2002] UKHL 32.

6.50 In *SO v LB Barking and Dagenham*[26] the Court of Appeal held that accommodation may be provided by a local authority under s.23C Children Act 1989 and further that Home Office support would not be available to a former relevant child who is entitled to leaving care support because:

> ...this court is, in my judgment, bound to conclude that since the powers under s.95 (and s.4) of the Immigration and

[26] [2010] EWCA Civ 1101

> Asylum Act 1999 are residual, and cannot be exercised if the asylum seeker (or failed asylum seeker) is entitled to accommodation under some other provision, **a local authority is not entitled, when considering whether a former relevant child's welfare requires that he be accommodated by it, to take into account the possibility of support from NASS.** [40] [emphasis added]

6.51 The conclusion that Home Office support is support of last resort, and therefore not capable of being taken account of by a local authority assessing whether some other form of support than leaving care provision is available, is also consistent with Home Office Guidance (non-statutory) issued by UK Visas and Immigration ("UKVI") entitled "Transition at Age 18" Guidance[27] (2014). This is an instruction to Home Office caseworkers and states that:

> Chapter 2 - Support Arrangements When UASC[28] Turns 18
>
> Many UASC will continue to be eligible for assistance from their Local Authority under Leaving Care legislation. A person will usually be eligible to Leaving Care support if he/she has been supported by the Local Authority for more than 13 weeks before their 18th birthday under Section 20 of the Children Act 1989 (Or under similar provisions in Scotland and Northern Ireland). **To note: A person who is eligible to receive Leaving Care support is not eligible for asylum support. This is because asylum support is a residual support entitlement that only applies if the person has no entitlement to any other form of support. If, however, UASC are not eligible to receive Leaving Care support they may be eligible for asylum support under Section 95 of the Immigration and Asylum Act 1999,**

27 https://assets.publishing.service.gov.uk/government/uploads/system/uploads/attachment_data/file/397101/Transition_at_age_18_instruction__Publicv4_0.pdf

28 Unaccompanied Asylum Seeking Child

provided they would be otherwise destitute and meet specific requirements. [emphasis added]

Applying to the Home Office to lift NRPF condition

6.52 One of the available "exit strategies" from local authority support is for an applicant to become able to claim "mainstream" welfare benefits. As noted in *R (Blackburn Smith) v LB Lambeth [*2007] EWHC 767 at para.36, the Children Act 1989 is not intended to replicate long term welfare assistance by way of mainstream benefits, and so an applicant who is destitute is able to apply to the Home Office for the NRPF condition to be lifted.

6.53 Home Office guidance (12 May 2021)[29] states that the criteria for such an application are that:

- since being granted leave to remain your financial circumstances have changed and you have become destitute, you are at imminent risk of destitution, there are now particularly compelling reasons relating to the welfare of your child on account of your very low income, or there are now exceptional circumstances in your case relating to your financial circumstances

- you were destitute, at imminent risk of destitution, there were particularly compelling reasons relating to the welfare of your child on account of your very low income, or there were exceptional circumstances in your case relating to your financial circumstances, at the time your application was being considered, but you failed to provide evidence of this and you now wish to send in this evidence

6.54 A person is eligible to make the application for change of conditions if their leave to remain is as a 10 year partner, parent or on the basis of private life rights, where the applicant claims that refusal of that application for leave to remain would breach their rights (or the rights of other specified persons) under Article 8 ECHR, or the applicant has leave

[29] https://www.gov.uk/government/publications/application-for-change-of-conditions-of-leave-to-allow-access-to-public-funds-if-your-circumstances-change

to remain on the basis of another ECHR right.

An applicant whose leave is under the 5-year parent or partner route can also apply, but if they do so, any future application for leave will be considered under the 10-year route, and accumulated leave to remain will not count towards a fresh application for leave to remain under the 5 year route. The Home Office regard a change of condition as resetting the clock for the purposes of a new 5-year route application.

6.55 Amendment to conditions of leave can be granted if an applicant is:

- destitute
- there are particularly compelling reasons relating to the welfare of a child on account of very low income
- there are exceptional financial circumstances
- the applicant is at risk of becoming destitute

"destitution" for this purpose has the same meaning as in s.94 of the Immigration and Asylum Act 1999 in relation to asylum support, i.e. a person is regarded as destitute if:

- they do not have adequate accommodation or any means of obtaining it (whether or not their other essential living needs are met)
- they have adequate accommodation or the means of obtaining it, but cannot meet their other essential living needs
- they are at risk of destitution if either or both of the above are imminent

6.56 The onus is on an applicant for a change of condition to evidence the financial and welfare need for this, and suggested necessary evidence includes information as to income and expenditure as well as a "*recent letter from Local Authority confirming that support is being provided*" and/or confirmation from any registered charity or other organisation providing support, and recent letters from family or friends who are providing support, giving full details regarding the extent of this and how often it is provided.

6.57 While there is no timescale for assessment of a request for a change of condition, it is stated that "caseworkers will make reasonable efforts to decide such requests promptly, especially those involving a child or an applicant who is street homeless, disabled or otherwise in vulnerable circumstances".

6.58 An applicant who is being supported under the Children Act 1989 and whose NRPF condition is lifted should then be referred to the local housing authority for assistance as a person who is homeless or threatened with homelessness (with their consent) in line with the Homelessness Code of Guidance (Chapter 4) and consistently with *R(Blackburn Smith) v LB Lambeth*.

Key points

- **An applicant who has leave to remain with an NRPF condition can apply to have the condition lifted**

- **This is a potential route into mainstream welfare support including benefits and housing assistance under the Housing Act 1996**

- **Change of circumstances must be evidenced, including destitution or risk of destitution**

- **Supporting evidence is required which can include confirmation from a local authority that statutory support is being provided**

CHAPTER SEVEN

WHO SUPPORTS THOSE WITH CARE AND SUPPORT NEEDS, THE HOME OFFICE OR A LOCAL AUTHORITY?

7.1 As was observed by Lord Hoffmann *Westminster CC v NASS* [2002] UKHL 38, [2002] 1 WLR 2956, "*there was a time when the welfare state did not look at your passport or ask why you were here … As immigration became a political issue, this changed*" [19-20]. Mainstream welfare benefits were gradually withdrawn from asylum seekers and those unlawfully present, and the loss of mainstream support resulted in applications to local authorities for accommodation and support under the predecessor to the Care Act 2014, the National Assistance Act 1948 ("NAA 1948").

7.2 This placed enormous pressure on local authorities and so the Immigration and Asylum Act 1999 created a scheme for central government to support asylum seekers and their families, with s.21 NAA being amended by the introduction by way of the 1999 Act of a new s.21(1A), which stated that overstayers and others, as defined, could not obtain assistance if their need only arose because of the physical effects of actual or anticipated destitution[30].

---

[30] Section 21(1) of the 1948 Act provided materially that:

"*… a local authority, … to such extent as [the Secretary of State] may direct, shall make arrangements for providing (a) residential accommodation for persons aged 18 or over who by reason of age, illness, disability or any other circumstances are in need of care and attention which is not otherwise available to them …*"

And s.21 (1A) stated that "*A person to whom s.115 of the Immigration & Asylum Act 1999 (exclusion from benefits) applies may not be provided with residential accommodation under sub-section 1(a) if his need for care and attention has arisen solely -*

(a) because he is destitute; or

7.3 There followed a series of cases concerning the demarcation between local government responsibility under the NAA 1948 and that of central government under the 1999 Act.

7.4 *R(O) v LB Wandsworth* [2000] 1 W.L.R. 2539 concerned an overstayer who had sought exceptional leave to remain on health grounds from the Home Office and applied to Wandsworth for assistance under s.21 NAA 1948. Wandsworth refused this, on the basis that an 94verstayer could not rely on the section unless illness prevented them from travelling. It was held by the Court of Appeal that on a true construction of s.21(1A), if the applicant's need for assistance was exacerbated by circumstances other than such destitution, then he qualified for assistance notwithstanding his immigration status. This case established the principle that the infirm destitute were the responsibility of local government in terms of accommodation and subsistence needs.

7.5 In *R (Westminster City Council) v National Asylum Support Service* the House of Lords decided that the role of asylum support under Part 6 of the 1999 Act was residual and that, when assessing whether or not a person subject to immigration control required care and attention for the purposes of section 21, it was necessary to disregard the potential availability of support under Part 6 of the 1999 Act.

7.6 *M v Slough BC* [2008] UKHL 52, [2008] 1 WLR 1808 concerned a Zimbabwean national who had arrived in the United Kingdom as a visitor and had remained following the expiry of his leave to enter. While in the UK he was diagnosed as being HIV positive. The local authority assessed his needs and concluded that he needed medication, which had to be kept in refrigerated conditions, and that he needed to see a doctor every three months. It concluded that, for the purposes of s.21(1)(a) NAA 1948, he had no need for care and attention, and so was not subject to a duty to accommodate him. Slough's second proposition was that should such a need for care and attention arise in the future, the contingent duty would be excluded by s.21(1A) of the Act because the

---

(b) because of the physical effects, or anticipated physical effects, of his being destitute".

need would arise solely from destitution. Thus, the core issue in the case was the meaning of the words "in need of care and attention which is not otherwise available..." in s.21(1)(a).

The House of Lords held that M's needs did not amount to a need for care and attention within the meaning of s.21(1)(a). "Care and attention" under s.21(1)(a) was a wider concept than nursing or personal care, and s.21 NAA accommodation could be provided for the purpose of preventing illness as well as caring for those who were ill. However, "care and attention" had to mean something more than "accommodation" because s.21(1)(a) was not a general power to provide housing. The natural and ordinary meaning of "care and attention" was "looking after", which meant *doing something for the person being cared for which he could not, or should not, be expected to do for himself.* It might include such things as household tasks that an old person could no longer perform or could only perform with great difficulty; protection from risks which a mentally disabled person could not perceive; or personal care such as feeding, washing or toileting. The looking after had to be of such a character as would be required even in the case of a wealthy applicant, and it was immaterial that it could be provided in his own home if he had one. The provision of medical care was expressly excluded. This was considered by the House of Lords to draw a reasonable line between the able-bodied and the infirm. There had to be some sensible flexibility and the primary focus had to be on present rather than future needs in order for the threshold into the s.21(1)(a) duty to be crossed.

7.7 In *R (L) v Westminster City Council* [2013] UKSC 27, [2013] 1 WLR 1445, the Supreme Court considered the meaning of "care and attention" and in particular the relationship between that and the provision of accommodation. It held that there must be a link between the care and attention and the duty to provide residential accommodation, see para.48 "the care and attention obviously has to be accommodation-related. This means that it has at least to be care and attention of a sort which is normally provided in the home (whether ordinary or specialised) or will be effectively useless if the claimant has no home".

7.8 The need for a link between the assessed "social care" need and the provision of accommodation has continued to be applied since the Care Act 2014 came into force. See *R (GS) v Camden LBC* [2016] EWHC

1762 (Admin) and *R(AR) v LB Hammersmith and Fulham* 2018] EWHC 3453 (Admin). This is notwithstanding the change from the concept of "care and attention" under s.21(1)(a) NAA 1948 to "care and support" under the Care Act 2014. Under both statutory schemes, a need solely for accommodation and/ or subsistence is not capable of triggering the relevant duty: see *GS* at [28] and *AR* at [19].

7.9 Guidance issued by the Home Office in August 2018[31] indicates that the Home Office does not operate a hard line between the infirm and able-bodied asylum seeker. It states that:

Local authorities (LA) are generally only expected to provide accommodation to asylum seekers if their assessment shows that the person needs the sort of residential care that LA adult services are required to provide. **An asylum seeker who has care needs which can be appropriately addressed in asylum support accommodation, and is otherwise eligible, should be accommodated by the Home Office** following a care assessment.

It will, in every case, be a question to be considered on assessment as to whether the asylum seeker requires "residential care" which may be a broader concept than the definition in the Care and Support (Ordinary Residence) (Specified Accommodation) Regulations 2014 [32] and potentially include other types of specified accommodation such as supported living and shared lives placements.

---

[31] https://assets.publishing.service.gov.uk/government/uploads/system/uploads/attachment_data/file/731907/Asylum-Seekers-With-Care-Needs-v2.0ext.pdf

[32] SI 2828/2014

CHAPTER EIGHT

SUPPORT FOR FAMILIES UNDER THE CHILDREN ACT 1989

8.1 Section 17 of the Children Act 1989 provides as follows:

> (1) It shall be the general duty of every local authority (in addition to the other duties imposed on them by this Part)—
>
> (a) to safeguard and promote the welfare of children within their area who are in need; and
>
> (b) so far as is consistent with that duty, to promote the upbringing of such children by their families, by providing a range and level of services appropriate to those children's needs.
>
> (2) For the purpose principally of facilitating the discharge of their general duty under this section, every local authority shall have the specific duties and powers set out in Part 1 of Schedule 2.
>
> **(3) Any service provided by an authority in the exercise of functions conferred on them by this section may be provided for the family of a particular child in need or for any member of his family, if it is provided with a view to safeguarding or promoting the child's welfare.**
>
> (4) …
>
> (6) The services provided by a local authority in the exercise of functions conferred on them by this section may include providing accommodation and giving assistance in kind or in cash.

(7) Assistance may be unconditional or subject to conditions as to the repayment of the assistance or of its value (in whole or in part).

(8) Before giving any assistance or imposing any conditions, a local authority shall have regard to the means of the child concerned and of each of his parents.

(9) …

(10) For the purposes of this Part a child shall be taken to be in need if—

(a) he is unlikely to achieve or maintain, or to have the opportunity of achieving or maintaining, a reasonable standard of health or development without the provision for him of services by a local authority under this Part;

(b) his health or development is likely to be significantly impaired, or further impaired, without the provision for him of such services; or

(c) he is disabled…

8.2 The duty of a local authority pursuant to paragraph 1 of schedule 2 to the Children Act 1989 is to take 'reasonable steps to identify' whether a child is in need. It is established that a homeless child is a child in need: see *R(Smith) v Northavon*[33].

8.3 As noted in chapter 2 above, the primary means by which a homeless person is able to secure housing assistance is via the Housing Act 1996. That route, however, is not available to a person STIC which may include someone who is not lawfully present in the UK[34], and also someone who

33 [1994] 2 A.C. 402

34 The adult in that situation may be ineligible for s.17 support by virtue of Schedule 3 NIAA 2002, but the Schedule does not apply to a child, and a human rights assessment may determine that it is necessary on article 8 ECHR grounds for parent and child to be accommodated together

has been granted leave to remain but with a condition that they do not have recourse to public funds ("NRPF").

8.4 The NRPF applicant with a family therefore falls to have a need for accommodation (and subsistence) assessed by local authority children's services. It has been held that Section 17 Children Act 1989 support is not meant to be a replacement for mainstream welfare support: see *R(Blackburn Smith) v LB Lambeth*[35]:

> the defendant's powers were never intended to enable it to act as an alternative welfare agency in circumstances where Parliament had determined that the claimant should be excluded from mainstream benefits;...

> However, in reality, and having regard to the fact that support under the CA 1989 can endure for the time it takes for the Home Office to consider an application for leave to remain, in some cases s.17 operates as more than a short term or emergency provision.

8.5 Once a family is no longer NRPF because leave to remain with access to public funds has been granted, children's services are required to refer the case to the local housing authority for support under Part 7 of the Housing Act 1996, in line with the Homelessness Reduction Act 2017 and revised Code of Guidance[36].

Is a child "in need"?

8.6 The principles applicable to an assessment of whether a child is "in need" are set out in *R (O) v Lambeth* [2016] EWHC 937 (Admin). These are set out at paragraphs 12 – 19 of the judgment and are summarised as:

(a) the duty of inquiry lies with the local authority

---

35 [2007] EWHC 767 (Admin) at [36]

36 https://www.gov.uk/guidance/homelessness-code-of-guidance-for-local-authorities/overview-of-the-homelessness-legislation

(b) there is a duty of disclosure as to relevant matters upon the applicant

(c) A failure to disclose relevant matters may, subject to procedural fairness, result in an inference being drawn which may be that the applicant has undisclosed resources: see *R(MN) v LB Hackney* at [45] and *O* at [21]).

(d) Procedural fairness requires that matters adverse to the applicant are put to the applicant to comment upon

(e) While a social worker is entitled to be sceptical in a situation where long-term support has ceased, a decision that a child is not "in need" must be based on something more than "feel" i.e. it must be evidence-based.

8.7 Whether in fact a local authority has complied with the duty to make inquiries and/or the requirements of procedural fairness is entirely dependent upon the circumstances. An examination of post- *O v Lambeth* cases is illustrative of its application[37]. By way of example, in *R(AA) v LB Southwark* [2020] EWHC 2487 (Admin) the local authority was found to have failed to make relevant inquiries because, having identified a need to gather information from the person with whom the

[37] *R (S and J) v Haringey* [2016] EWHC 2692 (Admin.)

R (OK) v Barking & Dagenham [2017] EWHC 2092 (Admin.)

R (CO) v Lewisham [2017] EWHC 1676 (Admin.)

R (AC) v Lambeth [2017] EWHC 1796 (Admin.)

R (U (a child)) v Milton Keynes [2017] EWHC 3060 (Admin.)

R (Stewart) v Birmingham [2018] PTSR 1204, Admin

R (AA) v Bexley [2019] EWHC 130 (Admin.)

R (SN) v Enfield & Haringey [2019] EWHC 793 (Admin.)

R(OA) v LB Bexley [2020] EWHC 1107 (Admin)

applicant had been staying, and with whom it was suggested she could continue to reside, the inquiry was in fact not sufficiently pursued.

Financial support for families

8.8 Where a family without recourse to public funds is supported under s.17 CA 1989, is there a minimum or specified amount of financial support which should be provided, and to what extent is this linked to other forms of financial support, for example by way of welfare benefits, or asylum support from the Home Office? In *CTM&U v LB Southwark* [2016] EWCA Civ 707 the Court of Appeal held that that:

(a) There are no categories or sub-divisions of 'children in need' in the statutory scheme. The assessment framework for children in need is one that applies to all children whose needs are being assessed, and there is no requirement for a local authority to have a specific policy in relation to children whose needs are related to immigration conditions [17-18]

(b) There is no "necessary link" between support under s.17 CA 1989 and support under other statutory schemes [22];

(c) The approach of the local authority, which was ot conduct a "bespoke" assessment of the needs of the family, with periodic review, and to take account of the entire package of support (including but not limited to weekly cash support) was a lawful discharge of the s.17 duty.

Family members of the child in need

8.9 Section 17(3) CA 1989 provides that "Any service provided by an authority in the exercise of functions conferred on them by this section may be provided for the family of a particular child in need or for any member of his family, if it is provided with a view to safeguarding or promoting the child's welfare".

8.10 In what might be regarded as the typical s.17 support situation, the reach of s.17(3) is limited to the parent(s) of the child in need, generally because the parent is able to meet the child's emotional needs but is unable to meet the need for housing or essential items. Support for the parent in that situation is a need of the child, as the parent is the means by which the non-material needs of the child are met. Human rights are clearly engaged in such a situation, with the parent/ child relationship clearly engaging article 8 ECHR.

8.11 The situation is less clear cut when the adult seeking support is not a parent of the child who is identified as being "in need" by reference to s.17(10).

8.12 In *R(MK) v LB Barking and Dagenham* the local authority declined to provide accommodation and support to an adult cousin of the child whose needs gave rise to a s.17 duty, the cousin being unlawfully in the UK. The assessment decision that there was no need on the part of the child for the cousin to be accommodated was upheld, and it was further held that the use of s.1 Localism Act 2011 was precluded by virtue of s.185 Housing Act 1996 as a pre-commencement limitation on the use of that power.

8.13 In *R(AO) v LB Bexley* [2020] EWHC 1107 (Admin) the challenge was to Bexley's decision not to make available financial support to the adult brother of the relevant child who was not, on the local authority's assessment, a carer of the child. It was concluded that whereas there was a power under s.17 to support family members including non-carers, this was limited to the situation where such support would meet an assessed need of the child. In that case, the lawful assessment was that the child's needs were met solely by his mother, and in that situation there was no power to provide financial support to the brother, as it did not meet a welfare need of the child.

Support for failed asylum seekers as a means of meeting a child's needs?

8.14 Not every asylum seeker with a child qualifies for support under the "main" Home Office support provision (s.95 of the 1999 Act) by virtue of the extended definition of an asylum seeker in 94(5)[38]. This may because the adult's asylum claim failed before the child was born, or before the child arrived in the UK.

8.15 In that situation, the family may present to a local authority seeking support and accommodation under the Children Act 1989.

8.16 Can the local authority in that situation have regard to the specific statutory provision which allows the Home Office to accommodate a failed asylum seeker (s.4 of the 1999 Act) as preventing the child (absent needs other than for accommodation and financial support) from being a "child in need" for the purposes of s.17?

8.17 That issue was considered in *(R (VC) v Newcastle City Council [2011]* EWHC 2673 (Admin). On the facts of that case, there had not been:

> ... the kind of detailed child-by-child assessment that would be required to justify the local authority's decision.

The question was identified as being:

> does the mere fact that support under section 4 is (or may be) available mean that without more ado – without any more elaborate process of re-assessment – it is open to the

[38] (5) If an asylum-seeker's household includes a child who is under 18 and a dependant of his, he is to be treated (for the purposes of this Part) as continuing to be an asylum-seeker while—

(a) the child is under 18; and

(b) he and the child remain in the United Kingdom.

> local authority to say that a child who was previously in need is now, *ipso facto*, no longer in need. [84]
>
> 85. That takes me to the wider issues which lie at the heart of this case.

As in Westminster CC v NASS and R(SO) v LB Barking and Dagenham, Home Office support was found to be a residuary power [86] with the result that

> … the mere fact that support is or may be available under section 4 does not of itself exonerate a local authority from what would otherwise be its powers and duties under section 17.

Insofar as s.4 had any relevance, it was limited to the situation where Home Office support under s.4 was both available and adequate to meet the needs of the child. As the local authority had not satisfied itself as to those matters, in particular by reference to a child in need assessment, that conclusion was not one which was available to it [95].

The "right to rent"

8.18 The "right to rent" provisions of the Immigration Act 2014 and impact on the "child in need" issue in the case of persons from abroad

8.19 The provisions of Part 3 of Chapter 1 of the Immigration Act 2014 include the "right to rent" which imposes a duty on private landlords and agents to ensure to check the immigration status of all tenants, lodgers and any other adult who will be living in the property prior to the commencement of a tenancy.

8.20 Section 22(1) states that "A landlord must not authorise an adult to occupy premises under a residential tenancy agreement if the adult is disqualified as a result of their immigration status" and by s.23, a penalty may be imposed on a landlord who acts contrary to s.22. The provisions of s.22 do not apply to an under 18, and are limited to occupation as the adult's main home.

8.21 Who has a right to rent? The right is given to those with British or Irish citizenship, those with indefinite or limited leave to remain or refugee status, and a person with pre-settled or settled status under the EUSS scheme.

8.22 The Home Office may also grant a time limited permission to rent. According to Home Office guidance[39]:

The circumstances will be very limited as the purpose of the Right to Rent scheme is to prevent illegal migrants accessing rented accommodation and to encourage them to pursue any applications or claims to stay in the UK from abroad...The granting of permission to rent is discretionary and is dependent on a migrant being compliant with requirements which have been made by the Home Office.

8.23 The same guidance states that:

> Permission to rent will normally be granted where any of the following criteria apply:
>
> - individuals with an outstanding protection claim, article 3 of the European Convention on Human Rights (ECHR) medical claim, or an outstanding appeal against the refusal of such a claim:
>   - relates largely to migrants who have sought asylum or made a claim for international protection
> - individuals who have lodged further submissions against the refusal of a protection claim and the submissions have been outstanding for more than 5 working days:
>   - relates largely to migrants who have sought asylum or made a claim for international protection

[39] Right to Rent: landlords' penalties V7 November 2020 https://assets.publishing.service.gov.uk/government/uploads/system/uploads/attachment_data/file/934469/right-to-rent-landlords-v7.0-gov-uk.pdf

  - particularly concerns protection cases where further submissions have been made ...

- individuals who have an appeal outstanding which cannot be pursued from abroad:

  - some certified decisions will not carry a right of appeal in the UK: other appeals which have been made in the UK cannot be pursued from abroad ...

- individuals whose judicial review application has been given permission to proceed and where the judicial review would as a matter of policy be treated as being suspensive of removal, this would continue until any reconsideration required of the Home Office as an outcome of the judicial review had been undertaken: o if a judicial review would not be considered to be suspensive of removal, then permission to rent should not be considered for that reason - for full guidance see Judicial review guidance

- individuals who have been granted bail by an immigration tribunal or the courts which contains a residence restriction and/or electronic monitoring restrictions...

- potential victims of modern slavery from the date of a positive reasonable grounds decision from the national referral mechanism (NRM) up until 2 weeks after either a positive or negative conclusive grounds decision

- recognised victims of modern slavery with an associated outstanding application for discretionary leave

- families with one or more children under the age of 18 who are cooperating with the Home Office's family returns process

- individuals who are complying with the Home Office's voluntary departure process: this includes those with genuine obstacles to return, providing that they are taking all reasonable steps to address these…

8.24 A checking service operates to enable landlords to verify whether a prospective tenant has a right to rent or permission to rent.

It should be noted that the right to rent provisions do not apply to the provision of local authority accommodation, presumably because there are in any event eligibility criteria for such accommodation.

The "right to rent" and CA 1989: if a family has resources, but no right to rent, is a child "in need" for s.17 purposes?

8.25 In *R(U) v Milton Keynes Council* [2017] EWHC 3050 (Admin) the local authority found the applicant to have withheld information as to her resources, and drew an inference of undisclosed resources from that. On that issue, the decision of Milton Keynes was upheld. However, the decision was nonetheless held to be unlawful for failure to consider the impact of the right to rent provisions on the ability of the parent, with (as found) resources, to use those resources to provide for her child's accommodation needs.

8.26 A different outcome resulted in *R(Stewart) v Birmingham CC* [2018] EWHC 61 (Admin) the Court, again upholding a local authority factual conclusion that the child's family had resources, was able to conclude that the permission to rent provisions provided a sufficient basis for the local authority to be able to be satisfied that renting was an available option for that family to meet the child's needs.

8.27 The right to rent provisions were found at first instance to be unlawfully discriminatory but that was overturned by the Court of Appeal in *Secretary of State for the Home Department v R (Joint Council for The Welfare of Immigrants)* [2020] EWCA Civ 542. The majority agreed that the scheme did cause discrimination on grounds of race or nationality, but that such discrimination was on the part of individual landlords, rather than inherent in the statutory provisions, and in any event the discriminatory effect was capable of justification by reference to a legitimate aim of maintaining immigration control.

CHAPTER NINE

THE LOCALISM ACT 2011

This is a general power of competence, allowing a local authority:

(1)... power to do anything that individuals generally may do.

(2) Subsection (1) applies to things that an individual may do even though they are in nature, extent or otherwise—

(a) Unlike anything the authority may do apart from subsection (1), or

(b) Unlike anything that other public bodies may do.

(3) In this section "individual" means an individual with full capacity.

(4) Where subsection (1) confers power on the authority to do something, it confers power (subject to sections 2 to 4) to do it in any way whatever, including—

(a) power to do it anywhere in the United Kingdom or elsewhere,

(b) power to do it for a commercial purpose or otherwise for a charge, or without charge, and

(c) power to do it for, or otherwise than for, the benefit of the authority, its area or persons resident or present in its area.

(5) The generality of the power conferred by subsection (1) ("the general power") is not limited by the existence of any other power of the authority which (to any extent) overlaps the general power.

> (6) Any such other power is not limited by the existence of the general power (but see section 5(2)).
>
> ...

9.1 The limitation on that widely drawn power is contained in s.2 "boundaries of the general power":

> (1) If exercise of a pre-commencement power of a local authority is subject to restrictions, those restrictions apply also to exercise of the general power so far as it is overlapped by the pre-commencement power.
>
> (2) The general power does not enable a local authority to do—
>
> (a) anything which the authority is unable to do by virtue of a pre-commencement limitation, or
>
> (b) anything which the authority is unable to do by virtue of a post-commencement limitation which is expressed to apply—
>
> (i) to the general power,
>
> (ii) to all of the authority's powers, or
>
> (iii) to all of the authority's powers but with exceptions that do not include the general power.
>
> (3) ...
>
> (4) In this section—
>
>> "post-commencement limitation" means a prohibition, restriction or other limitation expressly imposed by a statutory provision that—
>>
>> (a) is contained in an Act passed after the end of the Session in which this Act is passed, or

(b) is contained in an instrument made under an Act and comes into force on or after the commencement of section 1;

"pre-commencement limitation" means a prohibition, restriction or other limitation expressly imposed by a statutory provision that—

(a) is contained in this Act, or in any other Act passed no later than the end of the Session in which this Act is passed, or

(b) is contained in an instrument made under an Act and comes into force before the commencement of section 1;

"pre-commencement power" means power conferred by a statutory provision that—

(a) is contained in this Act, or in any other Act passed no later than the end of the Session in which this Act is passed, or

(b) is contained in an instrument made under an Act and comes into force before the commencement of section 1.

9.2 These powers, and their limits, have generated considerable judicial consideration in the area of local authority support for persons from abroad, in the context of applicants who do not qualify for support under housing, or adult social care legislation, or under the Children Act 1989, but nonetheless seek local authority support.

9.3 In *R(J) v. London Borough of Enfield* [2002] HLR 38 Elias J considered sections 2 and 3 of the Local Government Act 2000 (predecessor provisions to those in sections 1 and 2 of the Localism Act 2011) and decided that section 185 Housing Act 1996 (the eligibility provision) was a "prohibition, restriction or limitation" on the authority's power to provide accommodation to an ineligible person.

9.4 In *R (Khan) v. Oxfordshire County Council* [2004] HLR 41 the claimant sought accommodation and financial assistance from the local authority under section 21(1)(a) of the National Assistance Act 1948 (as discussed above, the adult social care legislation prior to the Care Act 2014) which included a restriction on the provision of support to a person subject to immigration control whose need for care and attention arose solely because they were destitute or because of the physical effects of being destitute.

9.5 The question arose whether section 21(1A) of the NAA imposed a prohibition, restriction or limitation within section 3 of the Local Government Act 2000. Dyson LJ referred, at [30] – [32], to the distinction identified in *J* between the definition of the scope of a power and the imposition of a prohibition, etc. on the exercise of a power. Dyson LJ explained that section 21(1A) prohibited any provision of residential accommodation to those to whom the conditions in section 21(1)(a) applied, as follows:

> 40. In my view, s.3 has the effect of preventing an authority from exercising the power in s.2 of the LGA to do that which is prohibited by s.21(1A). It is true that the phrase "under subsection (1)(a)" in s.21(1A) makes it clear that what is prohibited is the provision of residential accommodation under s.21(1)(a) for persons who satisfy the s.21(1)(a) conditions, but who are subject to immigration control, and whose need for care and attention arises solely because of destitution. Thus if (leaving s.2 of the LGA out of account for the moment) there were some other statutory power than s.21(1)(a) by which accommodation could be provided to persons who satisfy the s.21(1)(a) conditions, then the exercise of that power would not be prohibited by s.21(1A). But it is agreed that there is no other such power….
>
> 41 The effect of s.3(1) is to prohibit the doing of "anything" which a local authority is unable to do by virtue of any prohibition on its powers contained in any enactment. In the present context, the "thing" which is under consideration is the provision of residential accommodation to persons who, but for the prohibition in s.21(1A), would be entitled to accommodation under s.21(1)(a). It is that "thing" which the local authority is prohibited from providing by s.21(1A),

and which it cannot provide under any other statutory power, unless it can do so under s.2. But the very reason why s.3(1) was enacted was to prevent s.2 being used to do that which is prohibited by another statute. If Mr Jay were right, it would seem that no statutory prohibition would trump s.2 of the LGA unless it stated expressly that it was a prohibition for the purposes of s.3 of the LGA...

42 But as Mr Swift points out, to interpret s.3 in this way is inconsistent with the language of s.3(1) itself, which refers to any prohibition etc. which is contained in any enactment whenever passed.

43 So far as the policy consideration is concerned, I accept that s.2 has a broad purpose. The scope of the powers given by s.2 should not be narrowly construed. The local authority is given a wide discretion to exercise its powers to promote well-being. But the fact that s.2 should be construed broadly does not help in deciding the meaning and scope of a prohibition, restriction or limitation on the exercise of powers which is contained in another enactment whenever passed or made. It is clear from s.3 that Parliament did not intend to override legislative schemes that already existed. The prohibition contained in s.21(1A) of the NAA must be given its natural meaning. For the reasons that I have given, it cannot be circumvented by s.2 of the LGA. If the prohibition in s.21(1A) were trumped by s.2, the prohibition in s.3(1) would be severely emasculated and, at any rate in relation to pre-existing legislative schemes, of no practical effect, since they do not (and could not) refer to the LGA.

9.6 *R(Badu) v London Borough of Lambeth* [2006] 1 WLR 505 concerned an applicant for housing assistance under Part 7 Housing Act 1996 who was lawfully present in the UK, however his son was ineligible under s.185 Housing Act 1996, and could not therefore be taken into account in assessing Mr Badu's priority need (under s.189). The issue was whether the incompatibility of that situation with the ECHR, as upheld in the joined case of *Morris v Westminster CC*, could be averted by the use of other powers or whether there was a prohibition on the use of such other powers [60]. The powers which were said to be capable of allowing the local authority to accommodate included s.2 LGA 2000.

> The Court of Appeal held, applying *R (Hooper) v Secretary of State for Work and Pensions* [2005] UKHL 29, that a power to make alternative provision does not become a duty simply because the principal power is subject to statutory restrictions which are incompatible with human rights [70]. And once it was recognised that s.6(2) HRA 1998 was concerned with the preservation of Parliamentary sovereignty, the use of one power to circumvent the prohibited power would be a use for "an illicit purpose" and an abuse of power [71], see also [72]:
>
> > [A] local authority…is not obliged but… is permitted to use its alternative powers [in section 2] so long as … it does not exercise them with the object simply of circumventing restrictions – even restrictions which are incompatible with Convention rights – built into the impugned power…"

9.7 In *MK v LB Barking and Dagenham* [2013] EWHC 3486 (Admin) the Claimant, who was unlawfully in the UK, sought to be accommodated as an adult under s.17 Children Act 1989 or s.1 Localism Act 2011. She was ineligible for assistance under the Housing Act 1996. She relied on art. 3 ECHR either on a freestanding basis or, as in C's case, coupled with s.1 Localism Act 2011. In relation to the Localism Act argument, HHJ Bidder, sitting as a Deputy HCJ, held that:

- An individual does not do what C was seeking (the provision of accommodation and support): only a local authority did so [84]. Section 1 Localism Act 2011 was "*…not intended by parliament as a means of overriding a clear statutory scheme prohibiting the provision of benefits of all kinds to those unlawfully in the UK*" [84]

- It was impermissible to use the Localism Act to circumvent restrictions, even restrictions incompatible with human rights - per *Badu v LB Lambeth* [2006] 1 WLR 505 at [72]: [85]

- There was no free-standing human rights based claim to support on the basis of *Limbuela v SoS Home Department*, which was solely concerned with the construction of s.55(5)(a) of the NIAA 2002, as made clear in paragraphs 1 and 7 of Lord Bingham's judgment [89]

- Use of the Localism Act power would, in the circumstances of that case, be with the object of circumventing the statutory schemes (Housing Act 1996 and Children Act 1989) [103]

- The "safety net" power is s.4 Immigration and Asylum Act 1999

9.8 *R(GS) v LB Camden* [2016] EWHC 1762 (Admin)concerned a Swiss national who had, pre-Care Act 2014, been accommodated by Camden in a residential care home under the National Assistance Act 1948. Her care and support needs were re-assessed under the Care Act 2014 regime, and she was found not to have eligible needs. This was challenged and the assessment upheld: a pure need solely for accommodation could not be a relevant care and support need.

However, it was further concluded that there was a power to accommodate under s.1 Localism Act 2011. While s.1 Localism Act is, by para.1(1) (ka) Schedule 3 NIAA 2002 a prohibited form of support, that prohibition is of course subject to the need to prevent a breach of human rights (Schedule 3, para.3). In the circumstances of the case it was held to be necessary for Camden to exercise the power in order to prevent a breach of human rights by way of homelessness and destitution, as GS had no other means of securing accommodation and limited income. Notably, the Court was not taken to s.185 Housing Act 1996 as a relevant pre-commencement limitation, as discussed in the subsequent case of *R(AR) v LB Hammersmith & Fulham* [2018] EWHC 3453.

9.9 In *R(AR) v LB Hammersmith & Fulham* [2018] EWHC 3453[40] Upper Tribunal Judge Markus held, in the context of a claim that s.1 of the Localism Act 2011 permitted a local authority to accommodate a person not eligible under the Housing Act 1996, that:

> section 185 of the Housing Act imposes a prohibition on provision of accommodation under *any* enactment and not

40 https://www.bailii.org/ew/cases/EWHC/Admin/2018/3453.html

> merely under the Housing Act… The "thing" which the claimant asks the authority to do is to secure accommodation for him. Section 185 of the Housing Act prevents the local authority [from] providing that "thing" to the claimant, and it cannot provide it by way of any other statutory power unless it can do so under section 1… [29]

9.10 AR was followed in *R(Aburas) v LB Southwark* [2019] EWHC 2754 (Admin) at [23].

9.11 In *R(Ncube) v Brighton and Hove CC* [2021] EWHC 578 (Admin), the applicant was a homeless failed asylum seeker who sought accommodation from Brighton. He was assessed as ineligible for Part 7 Housing Act 1996 assistance, and subsequently obtained accommodation from the Home Office under s.4 Immigration and Asylum Act 1999. However in the intervening period, he challenged Brighton's decision that it had no power to accommodate him because of his s.185 ineligibility. The challenge was bound up with a series of letters and policies from the Ministry of Housing, Communities and Local Government under the heading "Everyone In" aimed at addressing the situation of rough sleepers at the start of the Covid-19 pandemic. It was concluded that powers to accommodate a failed asylum seeker could be found in Section 138 of the Local Government Act 1972 which gives "principal councils" additional powers during emergencies or disasters and in s.2B of the National Health Service Act 2006 (public health duties), neither of which were subject to any immigration related restriction or within the prohibited forms of support for Schedule 3 NIAA 2002.

On the issue of the Localism Act 2011, the Judge declined to "read down" the Localism Act 2011 to comply with the ECHR because human rights claims are fact specific and the insertion of words of broad scope risked going too far, and straying from the emergency health protection envisaged by "*Everyone In*". Particular reliance was placed on the fact that there was a specific statutory mechanism for the support of failed asylum seekers (s.4 of the 1999 Act) under which it was the Secretary of State for Home Department who was responsible, and who could be challenged if there were to be a breach of duty or delay in making provision where a duty had been accepted.

It was further held that the Localism Act powers do not have a "free standing" ability to enable the provision of accommodation.

Key points

- **The specific statutory scheme for those needing accommodation is the Housing Act 1996, which includes the eligibility condition at s.185**
- **The Localism Act power cannot be used to circumvent the Housing Act 1996 eligibility condition**

CHAPTER TEN

THE IMMIGRATION ACT 2016

Immigration Act 2016

10.1 Legislative provisions in the Immigration Act 2016 provide for a limit on the accommodation which central government makes available to an asylum seeker with dependent children. At present the definition of an "asylum seeker" at s.94 of the 1999 Act includes an asylum seeker with a dependent child, for so long as the family remain in the UK, and provided that the destitution criteria continues to be met, the family will continue to qualify for Home Office accommodation.

10.2 Provisions of the 2016 Act (not yet in force) change that, to allow instead for a 90-day "grace" period which begins with the asylum seeker exhausting all appeal rights. During that grace period, the asylum seeker is expected to leave the UK, or demonstrate that there is a genuine obstacle to them being able to do so. If a genuine obstacle exists, and an application is made within the 90 days, it is possible for a further period of Home Office accommodation to be provided.

10.3 So far as local government support is concerned, the provisions of Schedule 12 of the 2016 Act create a scheme whereby destitute families without immigration status will no longer be supported under s.17 of the Children Act 1989. Their support will come instead via a new paragraph 10A of Schedule 3 to the NIAA 2002. This is notable because the provisions of Schedule 3 currently in force are concerned with the *removal* of eligibility for support (including from a local authority). The new para.10A will confer a power to provide such support, albeit in limited circumstances.

10.4 The conditions for support are:

(a) that the family is destitute (applying the definition in s.95 of the 1999 Act, i.e without accommodation or the ability the meet essential living needs); and

(b) Have a dependent child; and

(c) Are not receiving, have applied for, or be eligible to receive, Home Office support for refused asylum seekers (discussed above); and

(d) one of the following applies:

- they have made a non-asylum application for leave to remain to the Home Office, which has not yet been determined, or
- they are in time to lodge a non-asylum in-country appeal, or
- they have a non-asylum appeal pending, or
- they are appeal rights exhausted and have not failed to cooperate with arrangements to enable them to leave the UK, or
- the provision of support is necessary to safeguard and promote the welfare of a dependent child.

10.5 The last criteria is indicative of the need for compliance of the new scheme with the provisions of s.11 Children Act 2004. It is difficult to conceive of a situation where it would not be necessary to provide support to safeguard and promote the welfare of a dependent child, where it has already been established by reference to the earlier conditions that the criteria for destitution are met, and that there is no availability of Home Office support.

10.6 Section 17 of the Children Act 1989 will remain the route by which other, non-NRPF categories of child in need are to have their needs met (including provision for their families).

10.7 It should be noted that at time of writing, the provisions of the 2016 Act as they relate to local authority support are not in force.

Nationality and Borders Act 2022

10.8 The Nationality and Borders Act 2022 received Royal Assent on 28 April 2022. It includes changes to support for asylum seekers (clause 12 of the Bill) to include additional factors relevant to the discretion of the Secretary of State as to the type of accommodation to be provided to the asylum seeker – specified factors including whether the asylum claim is being considered for a "declaration of inadmissibility" under the NIAA 2002, and whether the asylum seeker has previously complied with conditions.

10.9 Part 4 of the Bill concerns Age Assessment. Perhaps the most significant change is at clause 51 "use of scientific methods in age assessments" which would permit the Secretary of State to make regulations specifying scientific methods that may be used for the purposes of an age assessment in the case of a person STIC. The types of scientific method include the use of imaging technology (so, x-ray or MRI scan) and the examination and measurement of body parts, as well as analysis of saliva or cell samples.

CHAPTER ELEVEN

LOCAL AUTHORITY DUTIES TO A LOOKED AFTER CHILD IN RELATION TO IMMIGRATION STATUS

11.1 Where a child is looked after, the local authority acts as corporate parent to the child.

11.2 Volume 3 of the Children Act 1989 guidance is statutory guidance, and therefore guidance which a local authority must comply with unless there is cogent reason not to, see *R(Rixon) v LB Islington* [1998] 1 CCLR 119. Volume 3 is entitled "Planning Transition to Adulthood for Care Leavers" (last revised in January 2002). The mechanism by which a local authority plans for the LAC to transition to adulthood is the "pathway plan" which must be periodically reviewed. The guidance states that a local authority is required to **double or triple plan** for the potential outcomes of an unaccompanied asylum seeker's immigration status. 6.22 of the guidance states that:

11.3 Pathway planning for the majority of UASC who do not have permanent immigration status should initially take a dual or triple planning perspective, which, over time should be refined as the young person's immigration status is resolved. Planning may be based on:

- a transitional plan during the period of uncertainty when the young person is in the United Kingdom without permanent immigration status;
- longer term perspective plan in the United Kingdom should the young person be granted long term permission to stay (for example through the grant of Refugee Status); or
- a return to their country of origin at any appropriate point or at the end of the immigration consideration process, should that be

necessary because the young person decides to leave the UK or is required to do so.

11.4 While the guidance is specifically concerned with an asylum seeker, the same set of needs and therefore the same requirement to plan would logically apply to a non-asylum seeking LAC without established immigration status. That approach is consistent with the situation of the LAC who was the subject of the complaint in the Greenwich LGSCO determination (see below).

11.5 A failure to address the immigration status of a LAC within the care planning process is potentially a failure of compliance with the statutory guidance and therefore unlawful. It is also potentially recognisable as maladministration by the Local Government and Social Care Ombudsman[41].

11.6 Under the EUSS scheme, a late application (after the 30 June 2021 deadline) may be accepted where there are "reasonable grounds" for doing so. Reasonable grounds, according to Home Office guidance to caseworkers (December 2021)[42] include:

11.7 Where a parent, guardian or Local Authority has failed by the relevant deadline to apply to the EU Settlement Scheme on behalf of a child under the age of 18, **or where a Local Authority has failed by the relevant deadline to support a care leaver in applying to the scheme**, that **will constitute reasonable grounds for the person – including where they are now an adult** – to make a late application to the scheme. [emphasis added]

[41] See case number 13 019 106, a complaint against LB Greenwich, dated 16 January 2016

[42] https://assets.publishing.service.gov.uk/government/uploads/system/uploads/attachment_data/file/1041794/EU_Settlement_Scheme_EU_other_EEA_Swiss_citizens_and_family_members.pdf

Key Points

- A local authority acting as corporate parent to a child with uncertain immigration status is required in its care planning to address how the child's status is to be resolved

- At the point of transition planning for adulthood, pathway planning should consider the different eventualities of the immigration application and plan for each on a contingency basis

- The LAC may be prejudiced if steps are not taken while under age 18, because there is scope within some Home Office rules and policies for LAC status and the local authority plan for the child's long-term future to be taken into account in assessing whether leave to remain should be granted

- A failure to identify and meet needs relating to immigration regularisation may be unlawful and/ or maladministration

- A late application to the EUSS scheme may be made by a LAC or an adult who is a care leaver

CHAPTER TWELVE

COVID-19 AND SUPPORT FOR THOSE UNLAWFULLY PRESENT / NRPF

12.1 *R(Ncube) v Brighton and Hove City Council* (2021) EWHC 578 (Admin) concerned a failed asylum seeker who was rough sleeping and sought accommodation from Brighton. He was found to be ineligible for assistance under Part 7 of the Housing Act 1996, and had no care and support needs for Care Act 2014 purposes. He was, prior to the case being heard, accommodated by the Home Office under s.4 of the Immigration and Asylum Act 1999 (accommodation for failed asylum seekers), and so the case was academic, but its wider public interest resulted in a decision that it should nonetheless be heard.

12.2 The backdrop to the case was the "*Everyone In*" initiative from central government, aimed at protecting the health of rough sleepers, and preventing transmission of Covid-19. As noted in the subsequent case of *ZLL*, the central government initiative ebbed and flowed with tranches of funding from which local authorities could seek an allocation. The initial phase was concerned with getting street homeless people into accommodation, and the follow-on "*next steps*" programme was concerned with identifying sustainable move-on accommodation for those in temporary accommodation, with a view to preventing a return to street homelessness.

12.3 In the absence of the initiative itself identifying any statutory basis for those not lawfully present/ NRPF to be accommodated, and ineligibility for assistance under the Housing Act 1996 being clear, a key issue was on what basis a local authority could accommodate.

12.4 One potential basis was found to be s.138 Local Government Act 1972 which gives "principal councils" additional powers during emergencies or disasters. The conditions for the power to be exercised are that:

- there has been an emergency or disaster, or it is imminent, or there are reasonable grounds for apprehending an emergency or disaster;

- the type of disaster is one involving danger to life or property;

- if so, the Council is of the opinion that the emergency or disaster is likely to affect its area or some of its inhabitants;

- if so, the Council may incur such expenditure as they may consider necessary to avert, alleviate or eradicate some of its effects or potential effects.

12.5 The Court found those conditions to have been met, including that there was an emergency or disaster, notwithstanding the relatively low infection rates in Brighton's area, comparative to others (based on the then applicable tier system). This provision was held to be a power by which accommodation could be provided.

12.6 Alternatively, the public health powers in s.2B of the National Health Service Act 2006 were held to be capable of permitting the provision of accommodation. While this section sets out a target duty directed to local authorities to act to improve the health of those in the local community and does not confer an enforceable right on an individual, it was capable of empowering a local authority to accommodate. Use of the power in this way was not an attempt to circumvent the 1996 Act exclusions, and was not an artificial or strained use.

12.7 As discussed in chapter 9, while there was extensive analysis of the s.1 Localism Act 2011 power, the Court declined to find that this was an applicable power in the circumstances of this case, and in particular that the 2011 Act could not be used to provide accommodation because to do so would amount to circumvention of the eligibility provisions of the Housing Act 1996.

12.8 *R(ZLL) v Secretary of State for Communities and Local Government* (2022) EWHC 85 (Admin) was a challenge to the cessation of "Everyone In" brought by an unlawfully present (and therefore NRPF)

Chinese national who was a rough sleeper. ZLL sought accommodation from LB Camden, relying on *Everyone In*, and Camden declined to exercise its discretion to accommodate. His challenge to Camden's decision was stayed pending consideration of the above claim against the (then) SoS for Communities and Local Government.

A key finding was that *Everyone In* was not a policy but an "initiative" which ebbed and flowed with the course of the pandemic. In terms of the lawfulness of the initiative ending, it was held that this was political, and did not require publication or consultation.

12.9 The final phase of the *Everyone In* initiative ceased on 31 March 2022.

12.10 Whether it is appropriate for local authorities to exercise powers under the Local Government Act 1972 and/ or National Health Service Act 2006 will depend on factors which it is suggested may include local infection and hospitalisation rates as well as circumstances personal to an applicant. These factors may include the applicant's health related vulnerability, vaccination status and alternative forms of support, including central government support for current or failed asylum seekers. Limited public health resources may be a relevant consideration, having regard to the wide-ranging remit of public health provision.

Key points

- **Accommodation powers can be found in s.138 Local Government Act 1972 and s.2B National Health Service Act 2006, in specified conditions**

- **Those powers are not subject to an immigration status related eligibility prohibition**

- **They cannot be used to circumvent eligibility restrictions contained in the Housing Act 1996**

CHAPTER THIRTEEN

THE MENTAL CAPACITY ACT 2005

13.1 The Mental Capacity Act 2005 ("MCA 2005") is not primarily a service provision scheme and therefore unsurprisingly contains no expressly immigration related limitations. Nonetheless, there is clear overlap and interplay between the provisions of that Act, and those of the Care Act 2014, which are subject to the prohibitions and limitations of s.21 CA 2014 and Schedule 3 NIAA 2002. Welfare decisions on behalf of a P who lacks capacity to decide where to live are similarly capable of being impacted by available housing options which are limited by immigration status.

13.2 It may be possible for a person's care and support needs to be met by living in a sheltered or extra care housing scheme, for example, which offers a degree of inbuilt support such as a warden or alarm system in addition to any care package which may be provided. Application to such schemes are in many areas made via a local housing authority Part 6 Housing Act 1996 allocations scheme, and therefore are subject to the requirement that an applicant be eligible for the purposes of s.160ZA (see 2.2 above). It may be necessary for the applicant to be eligible for housing benefit in order to meet the rent. If P lacks capacity to make relevant decisions, the interplay of housing, community care and mental capacity legislation is easy to see in such a case.

Capacity to apply for status

13.3 In practical terms, a person may lack capacity to establish his immigration status or to make relevant applications to seek lawful status, in which case a person authorised to make decisions on behalf of the protected party ("P") (a Deputy of holder of Lasting Power of Attorney) or the Court of Protection may need to consider whether it is in is P's best interests for inquiries and/ or an application to be made.

Late application to EUSS scheme

13.4 Guidance to caseworkers[43] in relation to reasonable grounds for a late application being accepted states that:

Where a person lacks the physical or mental capacity to apply to the EU Settlement Scheme (or for example did so in the months before the deadline applicable to them), that will normally constitute reasonable grounds for the person to make a late application to the scheme or for an appropriate third party to apply to the scheme on their behalf. Where a person has care or support needs (or for example did so in the months before the deadline applicable to them), that will also normally constitute reasonable grounds for the person to make a late application to the scheme or for an appropriate third party to apply to the scheme on their behalf. This may include many adults with physical or mental capacity issues, but will also include adults with broader care or support needs, such as those who may be residing in a residential care home, or receiving care and support services in their own home, with long-term physical or mental health needs or a disability.

Availability of statutory services

13.5 The Court of Protection does not have power to direct public bodies to make available resources to an individual (*N v A CCG* [2017] UKSC 22) and it is limited to choosing, in the case of a person who lacks capacity themselves to make the decision, on a "best interests" basis, between those options which are made available by public bodies with statutory functions. The position of the incapacitated adult is in that regard no different to the person with capacity who would also be limited to choosing between those options which public bodies are willing to make available. The decision maker stands in the shoes of the person lacking capacity for the purposes of making the decision in issue.

13.6 In the case of a person whose immigration status attracts relevant limitations on availability of state support, those limitations will affect

---

[43] https://assets.publishing.service.gov.uk/government/uploads/system/uploads/attachment_data/file/1041794/EU_Settlement_Scheme_EU_other_EEA_Swiss_citizens_and_family_members.pdf

the available options between which the Court of Protection may choose on a best interests basis.

13.7 In the case of a person who is Schedule 3 ineligible and who therefore may not be provided with care and support save to avoid a breach of human rights, that statutory status will have an impact on the options which would be available if there were capacity to decide, and therefore upon the options from which the Court of Protection may select on a best interests basis. In practical terms, the relevant choice may lie between remaining in the UK with limited ability to access statutory support, or relocating to country of origin.

13.8 The position is different if services are not within the prohibited forms of support for Schedule 3 purposes, for example if there is an entitlement to s.117 Mental Health Act 1983 after-care.

Relocating abroad

13.9 In *UR, Re (Rev 1)* [2021] EWCOP 10 Mr Justice Hayden was concerned with the question of whether it was in the best interests of P to relocate to Poland, the country of her birth, where she had not lived for more than 30 years.

13.10 It should be noted that this was being considered in line with P's expressed wish to relocate, and not because of any limitation on access to support because of P's immigration status in the UK. P was not stated to be unlawfully in the UK, and the support she was receiving was pursuant to s.117 Mental Health Act 1983, so in any event not a prohibited form of support.

13.11 Nonetheless, the approach of the local authority in that case is a helpful guide in any case where relocation abroad is under close consideration, having regard to the fact that a local authority will be required as a minimum to ensure that there is no breach of a person's human rights, and that any relocation of a person lacking capacity to make that decision potentially engages articles 3 and 8 ECHR.

13.12 The judgment includes a list of factors are intended to be illustrative of the approach of the local authority in that case, and which therefore have wider significance in terms of the preparation of cases where relocation abroad is an option to be considered by the Court of Protection. The approach of the local authority in that case was described at [57] as a "beacon of good practice". The relevant steps taken and identified as a checklist for good practice were:

(i) Liaison with the relevant Embassy/ Consulate (in the first instance) to ascertain what guidance and assistance can be provided;

(ii) Evidence as to physical health to travel (GP);

(iii) Evidence as to mental health to travel (psychiatrist);

(iv) **Legal opinion regarding citizenship, benefit entitlement, health and social care provision in the relevant country, and such other issues relevant to the case**;

(v) Consideration of any applications that need to be made as a consequence of any legal opinion provided;

(vi) Independent social work evidence regarding the viability of the proposed package of care in the relevant country if such evidence cannot be provided by the parties to the proceedings or a direction under section 49 MCA;

(vii) Confirmation of travel costings from the commissioners of the care package, both in relation to P and any carers that may need to travel with them (who will pay?);

(viii) Confirmation that the necessary medication/ care will be available during travel from the UK/ for the immediate future in the new country

(ix) Transition plan/ care plan, to include a contingency plan and how the matter should return to court in the event of an emergency in implementing the proposed plan;

(x) Best interest evidence from the relevant commissioners;

(xi) Wishes and feelings evidence;

(xii) Residual orders to allow the plan to be implemented, including single issue financial orders regarding opening/closing of UK bank accounts, the purchasing of essential items to travel (if necessary);

(xiii) Covid-19 considerations prior to travel (if applicable) [emphasis added]

Key Points

- **The Court of Protection cannot on a health and welfare best interests decision alter or override restrictions or limitations on a person's access to support and assistance because of immigration status**

- **The Court of Protection can authorise an application for status being made on P's behalf if this is in P's best interests**

- **It will generally be in P's best interests for steps to be taken to resolve unlawful status**

- **Where relocation abroad is being considered, the Court of Protection will assess whether relocation is in P's best interests, and is likely to require evidence as to immigration status and as to access to health and welfare support in the proposed destination**

CHAPTER FOURTEEN

POWERS AND DUTIES TO THOSE WHO ARE VICTIMS OF MODERN SLAVERY OR HUMAN TRAFFICKING

14.1 This is an issue closely bound with both regular and irregular migration. According to UNHCR[44]:

When people are forced to flee, they leave behind more than just their homes. Being away from their familiar surroundings, they often lose their community support networks and end up being socially and culturally isolated. They lack access to basic resources and livelihood opportunities. Depending on where they flee to, they may lack a regular status.

These and other factors contribute to making refugees and other forcibly displaced people an easy target for traffickers, who prey on the precariousness of their situation to exploit them.

Many persons fleeing conflict, violence or persecution are also compelled to move irregularly to seek protection. For this, they often resort to the services of smugglers. In these circumstances, refugees are particularly vulnerable to being trafficked or to falling victim to serious crimes and human rights' violations.

14.2 Section 52 of the Modern Slavery Act 2015 contains the duty to notify Secretary of State about suspected victims of slavery or human trafficking.

---

44 https://www.unhcr.org/uk/human-trafficking.html

In addition to that duty, a local authority is within the list of specified "first responder" organisations authorised to refer a potential victim of modern slavery into the National Referral Mechanism ("NRM").

14.3 The threshold for such notification is "*reasonable grounds to believe that a person may be a victim of slavery or human trafficking*" and if a body to whom the duty applies has such reasonable grounds, there is a duty to notify (s.52(1)) but subject to the consent of a person aged over 18 (s.52 (3)).

14.4 Who is required to notify the SoS? S.52(5) lists those subject to the duty as:

(a) a chief officer of police for a police area,

(b) the chief constable of the British Transport Police Force,

(c) the National Crime Agency,

(d) a county council,

(e) a county borough council,

(f) a district council,

(g) a London borough council,

(h) the Greater London Authority,

(i) the Common Council of the City of London,

(j) the Council of the Isles of Scilly,

(k) the Gangmasters Licensing Authority.

14.5 In terms of the definition of a victim of slavery, this is aligned with the offence specified at s.1 (s.56(1)) and incudes conduct which would have constituted an offence under that section if that section had been in force when the conduct occurred.

The section 1 offence is defined as:

(1) A person commits an offence if—

(a) the person holds another person in slavery or servitude and the circumstances are such that the person knows or ought to know that the other person is held in slavery or servitude, or

(b) the person requires another person to perform forced or compulsory labour and the circumstances are such that the person knows or ought to know that the other person is being required to perform forced or compulsory labour.

(2) In subsection (1) the references to holding a person in slavery or servitude or requiring a person to perform forced or compulsory labour are to be construed in accordance with Article 4 of the Human Rights Convention.

(3) In determining whether a person is being held in slavery or servitude or required to perform forced or compulsory labour, regard may be had to all the circumstances.

(4) For example, regard may be had—

(a) to any of the person's personal circumstances (such as the person being a child, the person's family relationships, and any mental or physical illness) which may make the person more vulnerable than other persons;

(b) to any work or services provided by the person, including work or services provided in circumstances which constitute exploitation within section 3(3) to (6).

(5) The consent of a person (whether an adult or a child) to any of the acts alleged to constitute holding the person in slavery or servitude, or requiring the person to perform forced or compulsory labour, does not preclude a determination that the person is being held in slavery or servitude, or required to perform forced or compulsory labour.

14.6 In terms of who is a victim of human trafficking, by s.52 (2) this is aligned with the offence in s.2. The s.2 offence is committed if:

> (1) A person… arranges or facilitates the travel of another person ("V") with a view to V being exploited.
>
> (2) It is irrelevant whether V consents to the travel (whether V is an adult or a child).
>
> (3) A person may in particular arrange or facilitate V's travel by recruiting V, transporting or transferring V, harbouring or receiving V, or transferring or exchanging control over V.
>
> (4) A person arranges or facilitates V's travel with a view to V being exploited only if—
>
> (a) the person intends to exploit V (in any part of the world) during or after the travel, or
>
> (b) the person knows or ought to know that another person is likely to exploit V (in any part of the world) during or after the travel.
>
> (5) *"Travel"* means—
>
> (a) arriving in, or entering, any country,
>
> (b) departing from any country,
>
> (c) travelling within any country.
>
> (6) A person who is a UK national commits an offence under this section regardless of—
>
> (a) where the arranging or facilitating takes place, or
>
> (b) where the travel takes place.
>
> (7) A person who is not a UK national commits an offence under this section if—

(a) any part of the arranging or facilitating takes place in the United Kingdom, or

(b) the travel consists of arrival in or entry into, departure from, or travel within, the United Kingdom.

14.7 There is statutory guidance (updated 25 April 2022)[45]. The guidance states that:

2.8. To be a victim of human trafficking, the person needs to be subjected to the act of either:

- recruitment
- transportation
- transfer
- harbouring
- receipt

Means

2.9. An adult victim of human trafficking must have been subject to a 'means' – the threat or use of force or other form of coercion to achieve the consent of a person having control over another person.

2.10. The apparent consent of a victim to be controlled and exploited is irrelevant when one or more of the following has been used to get that consent:

- the threat or use of force

[45] https://www.gov.uk/government/publications/modern-slavery-how-to-identify-and-support-victims/modern-slavery-statutory-guidance-for-england-and-wales-under-s49-of-the-modern-slavery-act-2015-and-non-statutory-guidance-for-scotland-and-northe

- abduction
- fraud
- deception
- the abuse of power or of a position of vulnerability
- the giving or receiving of payments or benefits

14.8 The position in relation to child victims is different, however, because, as explained at 2.11 of the statutory guidance:

It is not necessary for there to have been 'means' for a child to be a victim, because children cannot give informed consent to engage in criminal or other exploitative activity, and they cannot give consent to be abused or trafficked. Any child who is recruited, transported, or transferred for the purpose of exploitation is considered to be a potential victim, whether or not there have been 'means', though in many cases the means will be present.

14.9 The potential victim who may have been trafficked as a child, but who was referred into the NRM only after reaching age 18, is assessed by reference to the child criteria for modern slavery i.e. they do not have to meet the means test. The potential victim must nonetheless consent to being referred into the scheme (guidance 2.12).

Adult or child?

14.10 Clearly this is important in terms of whether the "means" test is required to be met (see above). Given the issues which are capable of arising in respect of persons from abroad having no, or insufficient, proof of age, the issue of when a person is to be treated as a child, is relevant. According tot he statutory guidance, "child" is any person under the age of 18, and "where there are reasonable grounds to believe a person may be under 18 it is presumed they are a child unless and until their age is otherwise determined, for example, by an age assessment carried out by a Local Authority": see s.51 of the 2015 Act, and statutory guidance at 1.20 and 9.9. See chapter 5 above in relation to age assessments.

What information is required to be included within a notification?

14.11 This is specified in Schedules 1 and 2 of the Modern Slavery Act 2015 (Duty to Notify) Regulations 2015.

What happens when a referral is made?

14.12 A "reasonable grounds decision" is to be made by the competent authority, with the statutory guidance indicating that such a decision is to be made within 5 working days (14.48). This is a decision as to whether on the information available it is reasonable to believe that a person is a victim of human trafficking or slavery, servitude and forced or compulsory labour.

14.13 The statutory guidance at 14.50 states that the test that competent authority staff must apply is whether the statement:

> 'I suspect but cannot prove' the person is a victim of modern slavery (human trafficking or slavery, servitude, or forced or compulsory labour)'
>
> - is true; or
> - whether a reasonable person having regard to the information in the mind of the decision maker, would think there are Reasonable Grounds to believe the individual is a victim of modern slavery (human trafficking or slavery, servitude or forced or compulsory labour)

Support while a referral is considered

14.14 The First Responder is required by 15.5 of the statutory guidance to "make an immediate referral for the Modern Slavery Victim Care Contract support, including accommodation in pre-Reasonable Grounds cases where an individual is destitute or at risk of becoming destitute, is not eligible for Local Authority support, or where the available Local Authority support is not suitable".

Support available via the Victim Care Contract

14.15 A referral for support results in a needs-based assessment which is to address:

- physical (including sexual) health needs;
- psychological and emotional needs;
- cultural and spiritual needs;
- practical needs, such as but not limited to the need for material assistance, interpretation services;
- if there is a requirement to access legal advice and representation;
- if there is a requirement to access other advice and assistance;
- if any dependents should be referred to the NRM in their own right;
- access to education for school-aged dependents; and
- the production of a journey plan with the potential victim or victim.

14.16 Accommodation and financial support are capable of forming part of a needs-based package of care following a reasonable grounds decision, with emergency accommodation available together with financial support which is paid by the Home Office in an amount which is dependent upon the type of accommodation being supplied. Current support rates are set out in the statutory guidance at 15.37.

14.17 A positive reasonable grounds decision has two consequences:

(a) a 45-day recovery period is triggered. During this period, support and assistance will be provided (subject to consent) and there is a moratorium on removal action by the Home Office. This scheme was created to comply with EU Directive 2011/36 on preventing and combating trafficking in human beings and protecting its victims, Article 11 of which sets out obligations in relation to assistance and support for victims of trafficking

(b) inquiries proceed to consider a conclusive grounds decision (in relation to which there is no timescale, because it is dependent on the extent of inquiries).

14.18 The 45-day period of NRM support is capable of being extended by agreement of the Home Office: 15.154 sets out circumstances in which such a request may be granted, and they include the situation where the individual has the right to remain in the UK and is waiting for move-on accommodation to be made available, such as accommodation from a local authority.

14.19 A conclusive grounds decision is one taken by a competent authority as to whether, on the balance of probabilities, there are sufficient grounds to decide that the individual being considered is a victim of modern slavery (human trafficking or slavery, servitude, or forced or compulsory labour).

14.20 Annex F of the statutory guidance details the support available to adult victims of modern slavery. The starting point is likely to be an application for leave to remain, which is capable of being granted on discretionary grounds, taking into account the circumstances leading to the conclusive grounds decision.

14.21 Home Office guidance, "*Discretionary leave considerations for victims of modern slavery*" (10 December 2021) addresses the factors to be taken into account in considering such a grant[46]. Page 14 of that guidance makes clear that discretionary leave granted under that policy is not subject to a prohibition on access to work or to public funds. A person who is granted such leave should therefore have access to mainstream welfare support, including benefits and eligibility for housing and homelessness assistance.

---

46 https://assets.publishing.service.gov.uk/government/uploads/system/uploads/attachment_data/file/1040852/Discretionary_leave_for_victims_of_modern_slavery.pdf

Support for child victims of trafficking

14.22 The *Working Together to Safeguard Children* statutory guidance to children's services authorities identifies modern slavery and trafficking as potential reasons for a child being a victim of abuse or neglect, and therefore potentially a child in need as defined by s.17 (10), or a child at risk of significant harm for s.47 purposes. If those thresholds are not met, risk of modern slavery, trafficking or exploitation are factors which the guidance requires practitioners to have regard to in deciding whether there is a need for "early help" in order to prevent a child from becoming "in need" [para.6].

14.23 The guidance is clear that threats and risks to children can arise from factors outside as well as within the home, and trafficking is one such potential threat [para.40].

14.24 In terms of how an assessment is conducted, this is required to be in a "child-centred" way. This require that:

Anyone working with children should see and speak to the child: listen to what they say; take their views seriously; and work with them and their families collaboratively when deciding how to support their needs. Special provision should be put in place to support dialogue with children who have communication difficulties, unaccompanied children, refugees and those children who are victims of modern slavery and/or trafficking. [para.14].

14.25 Consistently with the Modern Slavery Act 2015, the guidance provides that a practitioner who has concerns that a child may be a potential victim of modern slavery or human trafficking should make a referral to the National Referral Mechanism as soon as possible.

14.26 In *R(H) v Swindon BC* [2021] EWCA Civ 1836 it was confirmed that local authorities are the primary service provider for safeguarding and responding to the needs of child victims of trafficking [42].

The issue before the Court of Appeal in that case was an alleged breach of article 4 ECHR[47] by the local authority, on the grounds that it was said to have failed to make relevant inquiries of the police and the single competent authority (the Home Office) about the risks to which the child victim of trafficking was subject.

Those failures were held to amount to a breach of duty under s.47 Children Act 1989. However, in the circumstances of that case, it was relevant that the child was being accommodated, and attended by social workers, teachers, support workers and health professionals. Analysis of the statutory assessment led the court to conclude that the child's needs and vulnerabilities were being met and considered by the local authority, such that he was being reasonably protected from the risks to which he was subject, while attempts were being made to recognise his own right to make decisions as an individual. In those circumstances, although additional inquiries could have been made, because of the level of support in fact being provided, there was sufficient protection from re-trafficking. The Court of Appeal upheld the judge's finding that there had been no infringement of the child's rights under article 4 of the ECHR.

Adult victims of trafficking

Local authority safeguarding duties

14.27 Section 42 of the Care Act 2014 requires a local authority to conduct a safeguarding investigation to determine whether any action

---

[47] Article 4 ECHR states that:

1. No one shall be held in slavery or servitude.

2. No one shall be required to perform forced or compulsory labour.

3. For the purpose of this article the term forced or compulsory labour shall not include: (a) any work required to be done in the ordinary course of detention imposed according to the provisions of article 5 of this Convention or during conditional release from such detention; (b) any service of a military character or, in the case of conscientious objectors in countries where they are recognised, service exacted instead of compulsory military service; (c) any service exacted in case of an emergency or calamity threatening the life or well-being of the community; (d) any work or service which forms part of normal civic obligations.

needs to be taken to prevent or stop abuse or neglect. This duty arises where the authority has reasonable cause to suspect that an adult in its area who has needs for care and support (whether these are being met or not), is experiencing or is at risk of abuse or neglect, and is unable to protect themselves from the abuse or neglect due to their needs.

14.28 The nature of the duty is amplified by the Care and Support statutory guidance, in particular 14.17. This provides that:

Local authorities should not limit their view of what constitutes abuse or neglect, as they can take many forms and the circumstances of the individual case should always be considered... Exploitation, in particular, is a common theme in the following list of the types of abuse and neglect…

14.29 The specified forms of potential abuse or neglect includes the following:

> Modern slavery encompasses:
>
> - slavery
> - human trafficking
> - forced labour and domestic servitude.
> - traffickers and slave masters using whatever means they have at their disposal to coerce, deceive and force individuals into a life of abuse, servitude and inhumane treatment

14.30 The safeguarding duty is within Part 1 of the Care Act 2014, which is within the prohibited forms of support and assistance for the purposes of Schedule 3 NIAA 2002, see para. 1(1) (n) and therefore potentially a form of support which may not be provided to an ineligible person, as defined by Schedule 3. However, it is arguable that an investigation is not a form of support of assistance, being a step removed from service provision to an individual. It should also be recalled that any prohibition on the provision of support is subject to the exception at para.3 of

Schedule 3, which disapplies the prohibition if, and to the extent that, the provision of support is necessary to prevent a breach of a person's human rights. Modern slavery falls within the potential scope of articles 3, 4 and 8 ECHR, and so it is questionable whether it would be possible to assess possible breach of human rights without the information about abuse, neglect or exploitation which may arise from a s.42 safeguarding investigation. The information would need to be ascertained, whether under the auspices of a safeguarding investigation or human rights assessment.

Care Act 2014

14.31 In terms of eligible needs for care and support, being a victim of modern slavery is clearly a matter of potential relevance to an assessment of need under s.9 Care Act 2014 and to the analysis of whether there are eligible needs for s.13 purposes. In and of itself, it does not establish an eligible need. Service provision to those STIC and/ or ineligible as defined by Schedule 3 may be limited by s.21 Care Act 2014 and/ or Schedule 3 NIAA 2002.

Localism Act 2011

14.32 A person's status as a victim of modern slavery may be relevant to an application for support under the general power of competence contained in s.1 Localism Act 2011. This cannot, however, be used to circumvent the eligibility restrictions contained in s.185 Housing Act 1996, and is a discretionary power, therefore capable of taking into account alternative forms of support (which may include support provided under the NRM).

Legislative Change

14.33 The Nationality and Borders Bill 2022 Part 5 makes changes relevant to the treatment of those who are actual or potential victims of modern slavery. These changes include the disapplication of provisions of the Trafficking Directive retained by virtue of the European Union (Withdrawal) Act 2018. The two stage process is, however, retained, with a reasonable grounds decision followed by a conclusive grounds decision. In relation to the recovery period during which the identified potential victim may not be removed from, or required to leave, the UK, this is set at 30 days, or the date of a conclusive grounds decision, whichever is the later, and may be disapplied in specified circumstances. A policy paper dated 25 February 2022 indicates that the recovery period may in practice remain at 45 days and that central government support as well as a moratorium on removal action will apply during this period[48]. A grant of temporary leave to remain based on an individual assessment and support to those in receipt of a conclusive grounds decision will be determined by a new s.50B of the Modern Slavery Act 2015.

Key Points

- **Local authorities should be alert to the possibility that adults and children presenting with support needs are potential victims of modern slavery**

- **The threshold for a referral is a relatively low one: "reasonable grounds to believe" that a person "may" be a victim of modern slavery**

- **A reasonable grounds decision under the NRM triggers entitlement to the recovery period, and the potential for this support to be extended at the discretion of the Home Office**

- **A conclusive grounds decision carries the potential for discretionary leave to remain without a NRPF condition**

- **Child victims of modern slavery should have their needs assessed under the Children Act 1989, with the risk of trafficking or exploitation being taken into account in relation to the process of assessment and services provided to the child and family**

---

48 https://www.gov.uk/government/publications/nationality-and-borders-bill-abuse-of-modern-slavery-protections-factsheet/nationality-and-borders-bill-abuse-of-modern-slavery-protections-factsheet

- In the case of an adult victim, the circumstances of modern slavery are capable of being relevant to whether and if so what care and support needs the adult has, and in relation to whether the criteria for a s.42 safeguarding investigation are met

MORE BOOKS BY LAW BRIEF PUBLISHING

A selection of our other titles available now:-

'A Practical Guide to Document Signing and Electronic Signatures for Conveyancers' by Lorraine Richardson
'A Practical Guide to Transgender Law' by Robin Moira White & Nicola Newbegin
'Artificial Intelligence – The Practical Legal Issues (2nd Edition)' by John Buyers
'A Practical Guide to Challenging Sham Marriage Allegations in Immigration Law' by Priya Solanki
'A Practical Guide to New Build Conveyancing' by Paul Sams & Rebecca East
'A Practical Guide to Inherited Wealth on Divorce' by Hayley Trim
'A Practical Guide to Shareholder Disputes in Family Businesses' by Ed Weeks
'A Practical Guide to the Law of Forests in Scotland' by Philip Buchan
'A Practical Guide to Health and Medical Cases in Immigration Law' by Rebecca Chapman & Miranda Butler
'A Practical Guide to Bad Character Evidence for Criminal Practitioners by Aparna Rao
'A Practical Guide to Environmental Enforcement' by Christopher Badger & Stuart Jessop
'A Practical Guide to Hoarding and Mental Health for Housing Lawyers' by Rachel Coyle
'A Practical Guide to Psychiatric Claims in Personal Injury – 2nd Edition' by Liam Ryan
'Stephens on Contractual Indemnities' by Richard Stephens
'A Practical Guide to the EU Succession Regulation' by Richard Frimston
'A Practical Guide to Solicitor and Client Costs – 2nd Edition' by Robin Dunne
'Constructive Dismissal – Practice Pointers and Principles' by Benjimin Burgher

'A Practical Guide to Religion and Belief Discrimination Claims in the Workplace' by Kashif Ali
'A Practical Guide to the Law of Medical Treatment Decisions' by Ben Troke
'Fundamental Dishonesty and QOCS in Personal Injury Proceedings: Law and Practice' by Jake Rowley
'A Practical Guide to the Law in Relation to School Exclusions' by Charlotte Hadfield & Alice de Coverley
'A Practical Guide to Divorce for the Silver Separators' by Karin Walker
'The Right to be Forgotten – The Law and Practical Issues' by Melissa Stock
'A Practical Guide to Planning Law and Rights of Way in National Parks, the Broads and AONBs' by James Maurici QC, James Neill et al
'A Practical Guide to Election Law' by Tom Tabori
'A Practical Guide to the Law in Relation to Surrogacy' by Andrew Powell
'A Practical Guide to Claims Arising from Fatal Accidents – 2nd Edition' by James Patience
'A Practical Guide to the Ownership of Employee Inventions – From Entitlement to Compensation' by James Tumbridge & Ashley Roughton
'A Practical Guide to Asbestos Claims' by Jonathan Owen & Gareth McAloon
'A Practical Guide to Stamp Duty Land Tax in England and Northern Ireland' by Suzanne O'Hara
'A Practical Guide to the Law of Farming Partnerships' by Philip Whitcomb
'Covid-19, Homeworking and the Law – The Essential Guide to Employment and GDPR Issues' by Forbes Solicitors
'Covid-19 and Criminal Law – The Essential Guide' by Ramya Nagesh
'Covid-19 and Family Law in England and Wales – The Essential Guide' by Safda Mahmood
'A Practical Guide to the Law of Unlawful Eviction and Harassment – 2nd Edition' by Stephanie Lovegrove
'Covid-19, Brexit and the Law of Commercial Leases – The Essential Guide' by Mark Shelton
'A Practical Guide to Costs in Personal Injury Claims – 2nd Edition' by Matthew Hoe

'A Practical Guide to the General Data Protection Regulation (GDPR) – 2nd Edition' by Keith Markham
'Ellis on Credit Hire – Sixth Edition' by Aidan Ellis & Tim Kevan
'A Practical Guide to Working with Litigants in Person and McKenzie Friends in Family Cases' by Stuart Barlow
'Protecting Unregistered Brands: A Practical Guide to the Law of Passing Off' by Lorna Brazell
'A Practical Guide to Secondary Liability and Joint Enterprise Post-Jogee' by Joanne Cecil & James Mehigan
'A Practical Guide to the Pre-Action RTA Claims Protocol for Personal Injury Lawyers' by Antonia Ford
'A Practical Guide to Neighbour Disputes and the Law' by Alexander Walsh
'A Practical Guide to Forfeiture of Leases' by Mark Shelton
'A Practical Guide to Coercive Control for Legal Practitioners and Victims' by Rachel Horman
'A Practical Guide to Rights Over Airspace and Subsoil' by Daniel Gatty
'Tackling Disclosure in the Criminal Courts – A Practitioner's Guide' by Narita Bahra QC & Don Ramble
'A Practical Guide to the Law of Driverless Cars – Second Edition' by Alex Glassbrook, Emma Northey & Scarlett Milligan
'A Practical Guide to TOLATA Claims' by Greg Williams
'A Practical Guide to Elderly Law – 2nd Edition' by Justin Patten
'A Practical Guide to the Law of Prescription in Scotland' by Andrew Foyle
'A Practical Guide to the Construction and Rectification of Wills and Trust Instruments' by Edward Hewitt
'A Practical Guide to the Law of Bullying and Harassment in the Workplace' by Philip Hyland
'How to Be a Freelance Solicitor: A Practical Guide to the SRA-Regulated Freelance Solicitor Model' by Paul Bennett
'A Practical Guide to Prison Injury Claims' by Malcolm Johnson
'A Practical Guide to the Small Claims Track - 2nd Edition' by Dominic Bright
'A Practical Guide to Advising Clients at the Police Station' by Colin Stephen McKeown-Beaumont

'A Practical Guide to Antisocial Behaviour Injunctions' by Iain Wightwick
'Practical Mediation: A Guide for Mediators, Advocates, Advisers, Lawyers, and Students in Civil, Commercial, Business, Property, Workplace, and Employment Cases' by Jonathan Dingle with John Sephton
'The Mini-Pupillage Workbook' by David Boyle
'A Practical Guide to Crofting Law' by Brian Inkster
'A Practical Guide to Spousal Maintenance' by Liz Cowell
'A Practical Guide to the Law of Domain Names and Cybersquatting' by Andrew Clemson
'A Practical Guide to the Law of Gender Pay Gap Reporting' by Harini Iyengar
'A Practical Guide to the Rights of Grandparents in Children Proceedings' by Stuart Barlow
'NHS Whistleblowing and the Law' by Joseph England
'Employment Law and the Gig Economy' by Nigel Mackay & Annie Powell
'A Practical Guide to Noise Induced Hearing Loss (NIHL) Claims' by Andrew Mckie, Ian Skeate, Gareth McAloon
'An Introduction to Beauty Negligence Claims – A Practical Guide for the Personal Injury Practitioner' by Greg Almond
'Intercompany Agreements for Transfer Pricing Compliance' by Paul Sutton
'Zen and the Art of Mediation' by Martin Plowman
'A Practical Guide to the SRA Principles, Individual and Law Firm Codes of Conduct 2019 – What Every Law Firm Needs to Know' by Paul Bennett
'A Practical Guide to Adoption for Family Lawyers' by Graham Pegg
'A Practical Guide to Industrial Disease Claims' by Andrew Mckie & Ian Skeate
'A Practical Guide to Redundancy' by Philip Hyland
'A Practical Guide to Vicarious Liability' by Mariel Irvine
'A Practical Guide to Applications for Landlord's Consent and Variation of Leases' by Mark Shelton
'A Practical Guide to Relief from Sanctions Post-Mitchell and Denton' by Peter Causton
'A Practical Guide to Equity Release for Advisors' by Paul Sams
'A Practical Guide to Financial Services Claims' by Chris Hegarty

www.ingramcontent.com/pod-product-compliance
Ingram Content Group UK Ltd.
Pitfield, Milton Keynes, MK11 3LW, UK
UKHW020145290926
15471UKWH00004B/705

9 781914 608247